T0316028

LEEDS ARE GOING TO THE PREMIER LEAGUE!

LEEDS UNITED SEASON 2019-20

PROMOTION IN THEIR CENTENARY YEAR!

Front cover photograph courtesy of Ella Spence

First Published in Great Britain in 2020 by DB Publishing, an imprint of JMD Media Ltd

ISBN 9781780916156

Printed and bound in the UK

LEEDS ARE GOING TO THE PREMIER LEAGUE!

LEEDS UNITED SEASON 2019-20
PROMOTION IN THEIR CENTENARY YEAR!

HEIDI HAIGH

HEIDI'S DEDICATION

This book is dedicated to my four grandchildren, Hannah, Laura, Alexis, and baby Freddie. Freddie was born nine weeks premature at the start of our centenary year and has proved to be a fighter and a good luck charm for Leeds United.

I also want to dedicate this book to our three legends: Norman Hunter, Trevor Cherry and Jack Charlton, who all lost their lives in the last three months, without seeing their dream of Leeds United back in the Premier League. Rest in Peace lads, you are back with The Don, Billy Bremner, other players, and Leeds fans in that special football team in heaven.

BLOG – FOLLOW ME AND LEEDS UNITED

Welcome back to all my followers for the 2019-20 blog *Follow Me and Leeds United* from me Heidi Haigh. I am a home-and-away season-ticket holder, a passionate Leeds fan of over 50 years and author of six Leeds United books. The blog is based on my travels to games and all views are my own and not meant to reflect on anyone else. I am happy for anyone to share these reflections with other fans and always try to respond to comments in good time. LUFC – Marching on Together!

AUTHOR OF THE FOLLOWING BOOKS:
Follow Me and Leeds United
Once a Leeds fan, Always a Leeds fan
Co-author with Andrew Dalton of The Good, The Bad and The Ugly of Leeds United, Leeds United in the 1980s
The Sleeping Giant Awakens, Leeds United 2016-17
Back to Reality, Leeds United 2017-18
Marcelo Bielsa's Leeds United, Leeds United 2018-19
Website: www.followmeandleedsunited.co.uk **Twitter:** @FollowMeAndLUFC
Facebook: Follow Me and Leeds United **Instagram:** Heidi Haigh - lufcheidi @followmeandleedsunited
LinkedIn: Heidi Haigh / **Group**: Follow Me and Leeds United

TABLE OF CONTENTS

Foreword   7

by Matt and Jack Brown, Dorset Whites

Prologue   9

Fans' Comments   12

Chapter 1 – July 2019   19

Chapter 2 – August 2019   27

Chapter 3 – September 2019   66

Chapter 4 – October 2019   92

Chapter 5 – November 2019   117

Chapter 6 – December 2019   133

Chapter 7 – January 2020   155

Chapter 8 – February 2020   174

Chapter 9 – March and April 2020   205

Chapter 10 – June 2020   216

Chapter 11 – July 2020   232

Chapter 12   245

Fixtures and results season 2019-20 – 54 games and final comments.

FOREWORD

LOYAL LEEDS UNITED FANS – MATT AND JACK BROWN, DORSET WHITES

I have followed Leeds United all my life, born and bred a Leeds United fan. Taking my son to a Leeds football game was one thing I was really looking forward to doing when I became a dad. Jack watched his first Leeds game when he was 5 years old. Since then he has been Leeds mad. We have followed Leeds through their ups and downs and have been season-ticket holders, travelling 600-mile round trips to watch every possible home game and most away games since 2016.

The atmosphere, excitement and joy Jack gets from watching and following Leeds makes this one incredible journey that neither of us want to stop. Jack likes to wait after each game, see the players walk past, and give them a cheer. The team, albeit ever changing, are always happy to have a picture taken with Jack and to sign anything he asks. It never seems too much trouble and brings him such an amount of joy.

He has an amazing collection of match-worn shirts from some of his favourite players. He takes his love of Leeds home with him from every game and shows it in his shrine-like bedroom. He has shirts from Dallas, Jansson, Phillips and Nketiah hanging pride of place, draping over his Leeds badge-covered walls. The most special shirt would have to be from Phillips, from an away game at Bristol

City. The first game of the centenary season. One iconic sad moment for myself and Jack was losing to Derby in the second leg play-off. We were all heartbroken that day, as all Leeds United fans were. To see Leeds go from strength to strength has been an amazing journey. Jack was just six months old when Leeds were relegated from the Premier League in the 2003/2004 season.

We are so excited for the season ahead and what is to come and hopefully get back to watching games post-COVID. What better time to get back where we belong, in our centenary year! Myself, Jack and our family have been through some unimaginable difficulties and sadness, and through this Jack's love for football has helped him get through stages of life most lads his age couldn't dream of. The love and admiration for the game and players help him focus on the positive aspects of our lives and the love of the sport. It is more than just watching a game for him. He can feel the excitement and the fun through the atmosphere on every visit to Elland Road. He can feel the support and spirit of all the supporters that we sit amongst at every game. They are more than supporters to us, they are all of us, Leeds United. MOT

LEEDS ARE GOING TO THE PREMIER LEAGUE!

PROLOGUE BY HEIDI HAIGH

After the gutting play-off disappointment at the end of last season, it was important that Marcelo Bielsa signed a new contract to stay at Leeds. Personally, despite not agreeing with everything that Marcelo Bielsa did last season, I believe he must do things his way. I am confident that he will get Leeds playing some fantastic football again and I am looking forward to following the team all over the country along with our faithful and loyal fans.

With the forthcoming season being the centenary year of the forming of Leeds United, could this be the year we finally get promoted? Leeds United won the FA Cup for the only time in their history in its centenary year, so it would be good to add another important milestone to our history.

Leeds started the pre-season friendlies with a couple of local games before a tour of Australia and Sardinia in July. Sadly, due to personal circumstances, there was no way that I could go to the games abroad. Although it was emotional not being there in person, the photos from friends and other Leeds fans who were made it all feel incredibly special. Once again, this showed the wealth of our worldwide support with local Leeds fans and over 2,000 travelling from the UK.

This book takes you on a journey to the games through the eyes of me, Heidi Haigh, the author, who goes to home and away games to follow Leeds United. The emotions, the highs and lows as a fan are brought to life through this pictorial journey following Leeds United. Never overconfident about our final goal, my loyalty to Leeds United never wavered and I support them through thick and thin along with many others. Fans love having their photos taken and being part of the *Follow Me and Leeds United* blog, with many fans feeling as if they are at the grounds beside me. Any fan who cannot get to grounds, and even those who attend alongside me, love to read the honest assessments and some of their comments are printed below.

Marcelo Bielsa and the Leeds United team stood up to be counted when it mattered and ensured they learnt from last year's mistakes. Everything was not sweetness and light, with the high and low emotions captured in the book, so enjoy the read. Did I tell you, Leeds are going to the Premier League!

FANS' COMMENTS

David Hill

Thanks for the photo Heidi and as usual a first-class report, always look forward to seeing them, MOT. Salford 13.8.19.

Allan Lana Stirk

Excellent report as always, Heidi, they always make you think that you are actually there and witnessed it yourself, keep them up. Salford 13.8.19.

David Robinson

Greetings from Singapore. Love reading your pieces – well written and better than anything in the normal press. Thanks for taking the time to do them, MOT. Salford 13.8.19.

Howard Crawshaw

Great read, thank you for being our eyes and ears and reporting on the games!!! It's so much appreciated. Wigan 17.8.19.

Beverley Smith

You're a great lady Heidi, what would we do without you, your blogs are amazing, and your photos are brilliant. You are sure one legend, all the very best to your husband and grandson, MOT. Wigan 17.8.19.

John Wafll

Heidi Haigh you were a great representative of the fans in the documentary as were all the others who contributed – it was superb. Looking forward to Wednesday – finally getting to my first game of the season and meeting my Leeds United family again – *Take Us Home: Leeds United*.

Dave Morris

Heidi Haigh great news about Phil and your grandson, what a week, even mentioned in *The Guardian* newspaper, don't let fame change you too much – *Take Us Home: Leeds United*.

Mick Glasby

You always give a very honest and fair account of every game Heidi. I love reading your post-analysis of each game. I said to fellow Leeds fans that although we didn't deserve to lose, some sides are going to get a real tanking off us when the ball in the right place goes our way. Leeds for eternity no matter what, and always Leeds and proud. MOT Swansea 31.8.19.

Diane Thompson

Thank you for your time and effort to give us your commentary and appreciate your words on the events at the game on the terraces. I love my team Leeds United and have done for 50 years. I don't like to hear that this kind of attitude on the terraces happens, but I only hope this is a one-off incident. Thank you again for your hard work to bring us your report. Barnsley A 15.9.19.

Gerard Collins	Love reading your reports and appreciate the effort … MOT all the way from Melbourne Australia! Derby H 21.9.19.
Gary Samwell	Bought today *Marcelo Bielsa's Leeds United*. What an enthralling read. I went to most away games and all home last season and what a descriptive recap of the season. Love the book.
Russell Rigby	As ever, best read on a Sunday morning Heidi. Three points Boxing Day and watch us go. Merry Christmas. Fulham A 21.12.19.
Nigel King	Heidi, I can't make it to most games now because of work so really look forward to your write ups so keep them coming. The longer the better personally, if I thought they were too long I wouldn't read them, but I love them, MOT. Fulham A 21.12.19.
Mark Jordan to Blackpool Whites Regional Members Club	Well done Heidi on her blogs throughout the year and thank you. MOT. Fulham A 21.12.19.
Steve Whitely	Love reading these, and even more so this one as I get a mention. Thanks Heidi the Book lady, so glad to meet and have a chat with you and your daughter, it was a pleasure to escort you to the ground, Twas a good night we did ourselves proud. I even got interviewed by Calendar after the game (if anyone has the fan interviews after the game please post for me), MOT. Arsenal A FAC third round 7.1.20.
Margaret Mags Musgrove	Great pics, and a great read, felt like I was there with you all. Reading H 22.2.20.
Mick Glasby	Yet another day in Paradise, Heidi. So many wonderful fans at the game. Lovely colourful pics you take of the LEEDS family. I met two brothers before the game who travelled up from Exeter in Devon and have been following Leeds for many years. Terrific match report Heidi which I do also enjoy reading besides the great pics. Reading H 22.2.20. Loved seeing so many different banners or flags Heidi and seeing loads of very colourful smiling Leeds fans. We all love Leeds, MOT. Middlesbrough A 26.2.20.
Jeff Way	Thanks again Heidi another great blog, let's keep this run going, MOT. Middlesbrough A 26.2.20.
Ilsf Andy	Another quality report from our roving reporter, thank you Heidi Haigh. Middlesbrough A 26.2.20.
Janet Gater	Thanks Heidi Haigh, a great write up and pictures as always. Middlesbrough A 26.2.20.

Andy Turver	Great write-up Heidi. It was great to meet you. You are more famous than many of the players. Huddersfield H 7.3.20.
Adrian Ochai	Fantastic day out. Thanks, Heidi, for your fantastic blog on this brilliant Yorkshire derby win. Also, I want to give a shout out to the awesome guys from Norway and Denmark who welcomed me with open arms in the Holbeck before the game. The result made the whole day worthwhile. Huddersfield H 7.3.20.
Bobby Joyce	Spot on match report as usual Heidi. To be fair to the linesman who came on as replacement to cheers, the boos for the immediate offside flag were more ironic than of frustration. It was a correct decision. Fans all over the country as well as worldwide as you say. Guys next to me had travelled from South London and Penzance! Huddersfield H 7.3.20.

CHAPTER 1 – JULY 2019

YORK CITY V LEEDS UNITED 10 JULY 2019 AT BOOTHAM CRESCENT

Welcome back to all my followers and I hope this season brings us the rewards we are all craving. Last season's ending hit many of us very hard and it has taken a while to get over not getting automatic promotion. We have brought Costa from Wolves who will have to hit the ground running for me, purely because I am not in favour of expensive loans, but as long as he plays for the shirt and stays injury-free they will be plus points. I'd been rather down due to Pontus Jansson being sold to Brentford this week, which had been preceded by Jack Clarke's sale then loan back from Tottenham. Instead of building we seemed to be dismantling what we had so I will wait and see what transpires on the pitch. At least it looks like we are getting rid of a lot of the fringe players who shouldn't be here.

Going to York straight away rekindled the passion of following Leeds for 50+ years in what will be our centenary year. As always, I make my judgements by what I see on the pitch but it was good to be back amongst our support with many familiar faces. It was also good to see that Nikki still had Rita her guide dog with her as we thought she'd been retired at the end of last season. Rita is a Leeds fan through and through who barks every time Leeds scores a goal.

Team for the first hour: Kiko Casilla, Stuart Dallas, Gaetano Berardi, Liam Cooper, Barry Douglas, Alfie McCalmont, Adam Forshaw, Pablo Hernandez, Jack Harrison, Patrick Bamford and Kemar Roofe.

Substitutes en masse: Robbie Gotts, Oliver Casey, Ryan Edmondson, Bryce Hosannah, Jack Jenkins, Clarke Oduor, Pascal Struijk, Kun Temenuzhkov, Rafa Mujica and Liam McCarron.

Leeds won the game 5-0, with goals from Harrison (3, 44), Roofe (22), Hernandez (34) and Forshaw (53). Attendance was 5,108 with 2,162 Leeds fans.

Leeds got off to a great start when Harrison put the ball in the net to give us the lead in the third minute after York failed to clear Hernandez's cross. Bamford had a shot over the bar but shortly afterwards was unlucky not to score when his shot hit the post. Harrison was playing well and his cross from the byline was met by Roofe in the box to put us further into the lead. Leeds were in fine form, not giving York much of the ball, and it was no surprise when we scored again after a great build-up from Harrison and Bamford, which enabled Hernandez to get on the score sheet. After a rare shot from York just before half-time that went over the bar, Leeds increased their lead with a second great goal from Harrison from outside the box. Leeds being 4-0 up at half-time had made it an enjoyable start to this pre-season friendly game.

The second half saw us carry on with the same team and Harrison was unlucky not to get a hat-trick when he was denied by their keeper making the save. Leeds did get a fifth goal when Forshaw chipped the ball over the keeper after being put through by Hernandez.

There was a mass substitution after an hour with only Casilla staying on the pitch, who became captain. Youngsters McCarron and Mujica were making their debuts for Leeds. There was no let-up in play as the youngsters carried on where the first team had left off, and I was impressed with the way they slotted into the way Bielsa wanted. The one player who stood out for me was young Alfie McCalmont as he played the holding role that Phillips normally plays in for the first hour. He didn't look out of place and has a bright future I'm sure.

It was nice to start off with a win, despite York not really putting up any opposition.

GUISELEY V LEEDS UNITED 11 JULY 2019 AT NETHERMOOR PARK

Leeds won the game 2-1, with goals from Costa (69) and Bogusz (80). Attendance was approx. 5,800.

Team: Bailey Peacock-Farrell (Kamil Miazek 45), Helder Costa (making his debut), Mateusz Bogusz, Kalvin Phillips, Ezgjan Alioski (Niall Huggins 86), Ben White (making his debut), (Nohan Kenneh, aged 16, 74), Jamie Shackleton, Jack Clarke, Leif Davies, Mateusz Klich and Jordan Stevens.

Substitutes not used: Bobby Kamwa, Stuart McKinstry and Theo Hudson.

We missed the build-up to the game as I had to wait for my granddaughter Hannah to get back from a school trip. We also had to pick our tickets up for the game from my nephew's house, which is near the Guiseley ground, so at least we had somewhere to park. We got into the ground just

as the teams were coming out so stayed at the corner where we arrived, with Hannah and Vinnie getting a place at the front of the stand.

It was a different team to York yesterday with more of the youngsters playing, but it was good to see Kalvin Phillips there. With all the rumours flying around that he was going to be sold, I'm hoping that's all they are as he needs to be in our team going forwards.

It didn't take long to see that Guiseley were going to be a different side to York as they were up for it from the start and were very quick on the attack. Phillips found this out when he was bundled off the ball and Peacock-Farrell was then beaten on a one-to-one to put Guiseley into the lead on nine minutes. Guiseley continued to put us under pressure and there was no free-flowing football from us that had been on show at York, which was a complete contrast to that game. It was taking time to get a grip of the game as we went in at half-time a goal down.

As we started the second half better, we thought Alioski had equalised, only for the linesman to put his flag up for offside. We should have had a penalty when our player had his foot taken from under him, and although the referee was poised with his whistle looking to blow, he decided not to give one. It took us until the 69th minute to get level on the night when Costa scored on his debut after some good individual work. Miazek, who had come on for the second half in place of Peacock-Farrell, was called on to make a save to prevent Guiseley from taking the lead for a second time.

Leeds took the lead for the first time after Shackleton and Costa combined to give Bogusz the chance to score. It took a few minutes for the scoreboard to update and we thought that Guiseley wanted to pretend we hadn't scored. Guiseley didn't give up but Leeds were able to hold on for the second win in two days.

As the final whistle sounded on 89 minutes, kids all over the ground ran onto the pitch as that was the sign for a pitch invasion. It was quite funny listening to the tannoy announcer pleading with everyone to get off the pitch, even saying he'd put a notice up on the scoreboard.

Even though this hadn't been a good game it was good for the players to start their build-up to the season. Unfortunately, Alioski went off injured and White was taken off with a knock. Let's hope long-term injuries are banished this year as that was our downfall last season.

I just want to wish all the fans going to Australia and Sardinia a wonderful and safe trip to either or both. To say I'm not jealous at all would be an understatement as sadly I am not in a position to go to any of the games abroad this year. I'm looking forward to seeing all the photos from those fans who are there though and see our fantastic support on show once again.

I'm now looking forward to the season starting in earnest on 4 August with our trip to Bristol City. Come on Leeds, we can do this! See you there – LUFC – Marching on Together!

CHAPTER 2 – AUGUST 2019

BRISTOL CITY V LEEDS UNITED 4 AUGUST 2019 AT ASHTON GATE

Welcome back everyone to my *Follow Me and Leeds United* blog that will take you through the centenary season for Leeds United. As a home-and-away season-ticket holder this will be done game by game, where you get an insight into an away day and lots of photos of the fan experience. Please feel free to share any posts or photos, but if you can give me acknowledgement for anything shared that would be appreciated.

For those of you who are already avid followers of my accounts, we will know shortly how the treatment of my husband's cancer has gone, but he is making good progress. Also, my baby grandson Freddie made a very early appearance yesterday (nine weeks before his due date), as he didn't want to miss all the action. His mum had a season ticket before she was born so I made sure he had his Leeds United kit ready for him to grow into before he was born.

With everything going on in the background with my family, I haven't had time to think too much about the new season but am saddened by both the Jansson and Peacock-Farrell sales. I know everyone is entitled to their own opinion, but I stand by my point of view that we should have built our team around Peacock-Farrell. Bringing others in on high wages to the detriment of players already here was always going to upset the applecart.

As always, I will make my judgements by what I see on the pitch. With Bielsa staying, that had to be the best news I wanted to hear as it brings the continuity I crave. Getting off to a good start will be key to how our season progresses, but being amongst our fans once again during our season's journey will be priceless. Make sure you ask for a photo when you see me if you want to be part of the blog. After a stop in Gloucester with lots of Leeds United discussions and good company, we arrived at the ground in good time for kick-off. It was great to walk down to the ground saying hello to lots of Leeds fans and seeing lots of familiar faces. The bottom tier of the stand was cordoned off, which is a shame as we could have sold extra tickets today no problem. As it was, most fans put their flags on show in this area, which was good to see.

Team: Kiko Casilla, Liam Cooper, Patrick Bamford, Barry Douglas, Stuart Dallas, Mateusz Klich, Kalvin Phillips, Ben White (making his league debut), Pablo Hernandez, Jack Harrison, and Adam Forshaw. Subs: Helder Costa (making his league debut) for Klich (76), Ezgjan Alioski for Douglas (79) and Leif Davis for Harrison (85). Leeds won the game 3-1, with Hernandez (26), Bamford (57) and Harrison (72) scoring for Leeds. Attendance was 23,553, with 2,126 Leeds fans.

After a few free kicks going Bristol's way, we settled into the game and there were some great pinpoint passes across the pitch. Casilla managed to put my heart in my mouth a few times again today with his charging out of the area runs. With one clearance in the first half, it went straight

to their player on the edge of the box, but Casilla made amends with a great save to keep Bristol out. Leeds started to look comfortable on the ball, and I was impressed with young Ben White, who was quick to show some nippy footwork, giving a good account of himself. We were able to keep a lot of possession and didn't look too troubled by Bristol when they tested us on a few occasions. The game turned on its head when Hernandez scored a fantastic goal at the opposite end to us on the half-hour mark to put us into the lead. I knew as soon as the ball left his foot it was going into the net. The Leeds fans had been in good voice even before the goal and upped the noise with great celebrations. We nearly got a second on the stroke of half-time when Forshaw's shot just went past the wrong side of the post – very close, but not close enough to score. The referee caused some controversy when Klich was fouled and stayed on the ground; he played on. When the same thing happened with one of the Bristol players, he blew up and stopped the game. Just remember, officials, I want a level playing field this season and not one rule for Leeds and one rule for everyone else. Also, when we are getting our shirts pulled right in front of the linesman, he needs to open his eyes because if I can see it in the stand then there is something wrong with his eyesight! I didn't feel unduly worried about Bristol in the first half as we played some good attacking football as we went into half-time with a one-goal lead.

The second half saw Bristol come out with more fight in them and it took a while for us to settle. It wasn't long though before Hernandez did some fantastic weaving in the penalty area on the left-hand side of the pitch and crossed for Bamford to head the ball into the net in front of us for our second goal of the game. I'd said before the game that if Bamford gets a goal, hopefully that will give him confidence to score more. We were on top at this point and looking good for a win. This was made even better when Leeds scored a third after a great counter-attack involving Dallas, then Klich, before Harrison put the ball into the net. With some fans singing we are top of the league, I thought back to last season when I wouldn't sing it in case I jinxed anything. I thought maybe it would be better if I were optimistic and just sang it anyway. With approximately 15 minutes left on the clock, Costa was brought on in place of Klich, which left us seemingly disjointed as we lost our prowess in midfield. This immediately gave Bristol the impetus, putting Leeds on the back foot and under pressure, so it was no surprise when they pulled one back, beating Casilla at the near post. With them then piling further pressure on us and coming close to a second, I thought we better not capitulate and let them get another otherwise we'd be in trouble. It took a while for us to calm down and get control again, but luckily we stopped them scoring another goal, so we had a winning start to our centenary season with a 3-1 away win. Hernandez got a deserved Sky man of the match with his magical jinx and fantastic goal, which was well deserved.

It was lovely to see Phillips coming over to the Leeds fans and handing his shirt over to young Jack at the front of the stand, who was really happy. This was also caught by the Sky cameras too, which was lovely to see. Apparently in the warm-up, the ball had hit Jack, and this was his way of saying sorry. Well done to both.

When we got back to the coach I went onto the roadside as a lad I know was being helped along the road but was in a very bad way. His injury looked really bad and the police were going to get a car to take him back to his coach, but in the meantime he was leaning on ours. Sadly, I had to get back on the coach as we were leaving, but I really hope he is okay.

We had a relatively good run back to Leeds and I was home in Halifax before midnight. After having really warm and dry weather on our way down to the game, it was a surprise to hit rain again on our way home. Our first home game of the season is the early 12.30pm kick-off against Nottingham Forest next week. It will be good to get back onto home soil, as this is the first time in many years we haven't had a home game in any of our pre-season friendlies. See you there, LUFC – Marching on Together!

LEEDS UNITED V NOTTINGHAM FOREST 10 AUGUST 2019 AT ELLAND ROAD

My granddaughter and I headed to Leeds for our first home game of the season as, for once, this didn't include any pre-season games at Elland Road. It was good to be back, having got in the mood for football by playing Paul Wilson's King of Elland Road song all the way from Halifax. We bumped into the 100 years of Leeds United documentary crew as we headed to Billy's statue to meet my daughter Dani but had to arrange to meet both my sisters there after the game. Due to car parking issues now prevalent at Elland Road, they were told they couldn't park in Car Park A as it was for VIPs only, even though there were plenty of spaces. Luckily, they got onto the park-and-ride site, but I know these parking issues have been felt very much by many of our disabled supporters.

I went to the Peacock as Dani and Hannah headed into the ground and stood talking to a Leeds fan I knew outside. As we stood talking, a photographer arrived to take our photo. It was nice to bump into Monica from the Philippines, who was over for the game, and also to hear that she enjoys reading my blog. I was also asked to take a photo of some fans over from America, with another one an avid reader of my blog. I managed to catch up for a chat with a few others, including Paul, one of my Selby Whites, and I want to thank my 'counsellor' for his support, which was greatly appreciated. After taking photos of fans I decided I wanted to get into the ground early to ensure my season ticket worked, although by the time I chatted to a few people I only got in just before the team came out. After hearing Bielsa's lookalike young Freddie from Ireland was going to be mascot, I also wanted to capture photos from him coming out with the team. When I'd seen there was a chance for other kids to be a mascot for the game with proceeds going to charity, I was all for giving my granddaughters the opportunity, until I saw the price. £750 per mascot is a heck of a lot of money and out of my league sadly, and many others too from what I read online. Elland Road was buzzing in anticipation of what this season would bring. With the transfer window now closed, our final signings for the season are French keeper Illan Meslier, aged 19 from Lorient, and striker Eddie Nketiah, aged 20 from Arsenal, both on season-long loans. We also lost Roofe, who

was transferred to Anderlecht, but the good news is that Phillips is here to stay, which is really important as he is the mainstay of our team.

Team: Casilla, Dallas, Cooper, Douglas, Phillips, Klich, Forshaw, Bamford, Harrison, White and Hernandez. Subs: Alioski for Harrison (73) and Costa, his home debut, for Klich (80). The score was 1-1 with Hernandez scoring the Leeds goal (59). Attendance was 35,453, with 2,001 Forest fans.

After one-minute's applause for those fans no longer with us at the start of the game, we attacked the South Stand in the first half. Leeds set off on the attack, putting some good moves together and also spraying excellent passes across the field. With an early appeal of a penalty after Forshaw was brought down in the area ignored, first Phillips with a save by their keeper then Douglas found his attempt blocked, as Leeds piled the pressure on. With numerous corners we couldn't manage that breakthrough early goal, but we did limit Forest's chances. Their keeper denied Bamford a goal when he made another crucial save. Forest had deliberately kicked the ball away three times without the referee even speaking to their players, which annoyed me. When Phillips brought their player down with a mistimed tackle, he was straight in the book as their player made a meal of it rolling on the floor. Stop being a namby pamby and be a professional with no play acting. When a similar tackle on one of our players didn't get their player a booking, I'm positive that was only because he got up on his feet straight away instead of rolling about on the floor. Dallas was body checked by their player on the edge of the box but didn't even get a free kick. Although we'd seen a lot of the ball and had loads of possession, we weren't able to make it count as we went in level at half-time.

It was nice to catch up with friends at half-time as Carole and I wished each other a happy birthday. I'd also seen Tony from the West Midlands who'd said the same. I said he never looked a day older than when I first met him all those years ago in the seventies.

I hoped we'd be able to get on top of things in the second half as we attacked the Kop. Bamford came close twice with one shot off the crossbar and another effort needing a bit more power on it as his chip went wide. Once he starts scoring at home, I'm sure the goals will come. He is putting more effort into his game now and just needs to up his confidence. There may be large expectations when playing at Elland Road, but he couldn't fault the crowd for getting behind him. Forest had a rare attack, but the ball went over the crossbar. Suddenly, Klich put a fantastic ball over the top of their defence for Hernandez to run onto and I knew he would score. As the ball hit the back of the net, Elland Road erupted as a blue flare was let off in the Kop. In the pandemonium, I saw stewards at the front of the Kop motioning for assistance so I thought someone must be hurt. Eventually they were stretchered out of the ground, but hopefully they weren't too badly hurt.

As Forest brought on their three subs early in the second half (although at different times), I couldn't help but notice the size of them. It was like David and Goliath when I saw their players against ours. This also came to haunt us when they won a corner in front of the South Stand. In the melee the ball was eventually put into our net for them to equalise. Although I haven't seen

it, others said Cooper had been fouled in the build-up to the goal, but it was allowed to stand. My husband confirmed this when I got home too as well as confirming we should have had two penalties. One where Costa had three of them on him in the penalty area probably wasn't one from my point of view, but another where he was brought down was a cast-iron one conveniently ignored by the referee. Cooper had a push in the back which was ignored too. He went for the ball then ended up a few feet away from where he jumped so that was blatant to me. The bad foul on Dallas was even worse but ignored by the referee too. There were many bad fouls from Forest, and it looks like our team are going to face a battering again this season. When teams can't beat us, they will not hesitate to foul us instead. Some of them should have been bookings but luckily for them the referee let them off.

Once again, the referee was very poor in many aspects and the officials should be accountable for their inaction. He went off at the end of the game with the Kop booing and giving him stick for his inept display on the pitch. Although it was disappointing not to get all three points, at least we won't have other clubs baying to claim the end of our unbeaten run.

We met up with my sisters Karin and Erica at Billy's statue before heading home. Luckily, we managed to get away easily, although we didn't go straight home. Hannah sent a tweet to Susan Smith after the game as she'd broken down and didn't manage to get to the game. She'd been looking forward to getting a photo with her but that will have to be at the next game instead.

Tuesday sees our Carabao Cup tie at Salford, which will be a new ground for me, before the away game at Wigan next Saturday. Our away following will be contrasting at both games as we have only a small allocation of tickets for the former with approximately 5,000 for Wigan. See you there – LUFC – Marching on Together!

SALFORD CITY V LEEDS UNITED 13 AUGUST 2019
CARABAO CUP FIRST ROUND AT THE PENINSULA STADIUM

With a new ground to visit on the horizon, I was looking forward to the game. Although there would be a lot of changes to the team from Saturday, it was a chance to see our fringe players in action, including our latest signings in Costa and Nketiah. As someone who wants us to progress in the cups as winning breeds winning in my eyes, I didn't want any banana skins tonight but a progression to the next round. With it only being a short journey over the Pennines, we got there before the gates had even opened, but luckily we didn't have long to wait before we were let in. Everyone was searched before being allowed in, but I think some things were way over the top. When I saw one of our disabled fans being patted down, I shook my head. The lady who searched me laughed at all my bags etc. but I even had to open my water bottle to prove it was water. Another lad was asked to open his wallet! Apparently, they were looking for drugs.

I hung my flag up at the front of the barriers because I knew they wouldn't be allowed along the perimeter due to advertising hoardings. We had plenty of flags on show as usual, and with so

many familiar faces there I had loads saying hello or asking for photos. It's always nice to have a chat with many of our fans who I saw today, but I'm biased when I say we have the best fans in the world. There had been a lot of hype for this game by Sky as they were doing a documentary on Salford City due to the involvement of ex-man u player Gary Neville and others. There is only one class of 92 and that was Howard Wilkinson's Leeds United who won the First Division, making us the last champions before the invention of the Premier League!

The team: Casilla, Berardi (captain), Phillips, Davis, Costa (first start), Eddie Nketiah (making his debut), Clarke, Shackleton, White, Klich and Alioski. Subs: Alfie McCalmont (making his debut) for Clarke (70), Harrison for Alioski (78) and Bamford for Nketiah (78). Attendance was a sell-out 5,108, with 1,400 Leeds fans. Leeds won the game 3-0 with goals from Nketiah (43), Berardi (50) and Klich (58).

The first half saw Casilla tested early on before Phillips found his shot sailing way off target. It was worth a try especially as we were building up very slowly in our attacks. We had Davis to thank for keeping Salford out from a corner with a goal-line clearance with Casilla beaten. We looked very shaky at that moment as defending corners once again nearly came to haunt us. It was only when Salford attacked us that I realised how tall their players were. With one corner Alioski looked like he was going to try and mark one of them, which would have been another David and Goliath show. Luckily, the other players made sure White got to mark him instead. I've no idea why other teams always seem to have giants in them. Phillips's next effort brought a great save out of their keeper

and shortly afterwards he (Neal) prevented him scoring again. Salford always looked dangerous on the break when they were running towards us but Casilla did well to make the save to prevent them taking the lead. Clarke was the next one unlucky not to score when Neal saved a long-range shot from him. Although we had a few chances we had kept the tempo low and I said it was like watching paint dry and we needed to up it. Just before half-time we did just that, when Shackleton sent a great pass out to Costa who beat his man at the by-line, sending a great cross for Nketiah to get a goal on his debut. Klich was very unlucky not to get us a second before the break as his shot went past the wrong side of the post. The goal was just what we needed going into the second half.

Having got the vital break of a goal, we only had to wait five minutes in the second half to get another. This time Berardi scored his second goal for Leeds when he got on the end of a corner to beat Neal to put us two-up on the night. He ran straight back to the other end to celebrate, probably because when he got his first goal at Newport he got booked for celebrating with the Leeds fans. Klich came close to giving Leeds a third when he should have kept the ball down but volleyed it over. Casilla then made two great saves to deny Salford the chance to get back into the game. Leeds then broke free from the corner and came charging towards the Leeds fans with Klich in the driving seat. He kept going and sent a fantastic shot into the top corner of the net to send the Leeds fans into overdrive, especially in the no man's land in front of the barriers! We had Casilla to thank for another save before Berardi made our second goal-line clearance to keep Salford out. Luckily, they were unable to score from a rebound with the goal at their mercy after another Casilla save. Keeping a clean sheet and getting a 3-0 win was good to see and now we meet Stoke at Elland Road the week after we play them away in the league.

When one of their fans ran onto the pitch and went to score, he slipped and missed, which had the Leeds fans jeering at him. As he slipped back into the crowd, his jacket was thrown back onto the pitch as he mingled with their fans. Surprise, surprise though, he wasn't challenged at all by their stewards. There again those at our end did try to move our fans out of the no-man's land after our second goal but gave up rather quickly. He was the second fan to end up on his backside as one going out at half-time to the left of us was trying to be clever and fell over too. Must be something in the water over there! One thing I didn't hear until after the game was Salford fans mocking the deaths of our two lads in Turkey. I've no time for imbeciles like that and, although not a violent person, would love them to get their comeuppance!

Saturday sees us back in league action with the away game at Wigan, where we have a big following of over 5,000 fans. Keep scoring goals Leeds and get us another win. See you there – LUFC – Marching on Together!

WIGAN V LEEDS UNITED 17 AUGUST 2019 AT THE DW STADIUM

Well it's been quite a week. Wednesday saw me attend the premiere event for the documentary *Take Us Home: Leeds United* at the Everyman Cinema in the Trinity Centre, Leeds. I got a VIP invitation because I featured in the documentary and it was a great opportunity to be involved. My grateful thanks go to all those who made this possible for me. Please note though, it should have been a blue carpet as we don't do red! I watched the remaining five episodes last night and had to keep watching until the end no matter how painful it was at times. I found it very emotional but did enjoy it because this is Leeds United, my football club and fellow supporters. I would like to say a big thank you to everyone who took their time today to compliment me on my performance in this or asked for their photo to be taken. As always, I appreciate all your comments.

For those of you who have been following my family challenges since the beginning of the year, finally we have some good news to focus on. My husband's latest tests are fine, and any residual changes are down to the treatment he has had for his cancer. Huddersfield Royal Infirmary will be keeping an eye on him for the next five years. I know we're not the only people who have been going through this and good luck to any other Leeds fans/family who are going through similar challenges. My baby grandson is making good progress and should be transferred into special care shortly rather than being in intensive care. He is now over 3lbs and putting weight on, which is good to see.

Team: Casilla, Douglas, Cooper, White, Dallas, Phillips, Hernandez, Klich, Forshaw, Harrison and Bamford. Subs: Costa for Klich (76) and Shackleton for Forshaw (90). Attendance was 14,819, with 5,200 Leeds fans. Leeds won 2-0 with a brace from Bamford (34 and 65).

As I got in my car to head to Leeds, the heavens opened, and I thought we'd be in for another soggy day. It was nice to see the sun begin to shine when I got to the ground, and luckily for us it stayed out all day, plus it was quite warm. After ending up with freezing fingers at Salford during the week, it was a very welcome change to the weather. It was nice to meet Dean from Leyland during our pub stop and hopefully he managed to get into the ground. After getting a coffee I found myself in the bad books as I knocked it over, soaking my daughter Dani with hot liquid as well as me. She wasn't impressed with me and said I can't be taken anywhere! We got to the ground with plenty of time to kick-off, and as we made our way to the front of the stand, it looked like I wasn't going to be able to put my flag up. As Dani and I made our way to the front corner, we managed to hang it over the end of the stand. At that moment it was so blustery I was expecting the wind to take off with it so made extra sure that it was tied on tight.

There was a good atmosphere under the stand as I made my way back into the middle section to my seat. I was right behind the goal but had a great view. The atmosphere transferred itself onto the terraces, which was great as I really enjoy the singing. It was good to see that Sean had made it to the game, travelling from Australia. The first half started slowly, and Wigan were at their most dangerous at this time. With Casilla chasing after the ball back towards the goal, I shouted at him to pick the damn ball up. Obviously, I was nervous at that time as I swore at him too. Sorry about that. He made amends for me just after that when he made a good save to keep Wigan out. When Wigan hit the post, we were able to clear the ball as we gradually began to take charge of the game.

Wigan were doing their damndest to stop our players by fouling them, with some challenges going unpunished, but also getting quite a few free kicks. I said to the lad next to me that we don't want them going down to ten men this time as we know what happened at Elland Road last season. With Wigan's next attack, the referee blew for a free kick to them for a foul just before Bamford received a really bad one from their player who had already been booked. The next minute, after what seemed to be a message from his linesman to the left of us, he changed his mind and gave their player a second yellow then a red card. With Wigan down to ten men once again, I thought we'd make sure we didn't succumb to them in the same way as we did at Elland Road. Learn from your mistakes came to mind. Bamford hit a weak shot at goal when he should have put some power behind it. I said he needed some lessons from Allan Clarke on how to turn any attempts into goals. Once he learns from him, he'll do better. A few minutes later he did indeed score as Forshaw's shot rebounded off the post for Bamford to stick the ball into the net out of reach of their keeper. It was good to get the goal and put us in front on the day. Just after that fighting broke out in the main stand to our right as Leeds fans were under attack. I wasn't sure if it was some of our corporate fans, as I thought I saw some wearing lanyards who were then taken out through one of the boxes. Hopefully, no one was badly hurt. Just before the break Hernandez had a shot saved, meaning we went in a goal up at half-time.

It took ages to get underneath the stand to the far end where the ladies were situated. It wasn't a surprise to see a few of the lads obviously can't read when they were challenged about why they were in there. As I made my way back to the middle of the stand, I bumped into Ella before someone knocked some of her beer out of her hand. The next minute the same thing happened again before someone stood next to me found the same happened to him. The next minute we ended up with a beer bath as some was thrown into the air. Dani said it was karma when I told her later, saying I couldn't complain after spilling my coffee on her lol. By the time I got back in the stand the game had already kicked off.

The second half started with lots of free kicks given to both sides with many stop and starts. Wigan shouted for a penalty when challenged in the area, but the referee waved play on. I didn't think it warranted one though. When Leeds whipped the ball off the toes of a Wigan player, we were all mystified when they were awarded a free kick as it looked like a perfectly legitimate challenge to us. Leeds were awarded a corner, with many Leeds fans going mad that we should have had a penalty for handball. With the new rule changes, a penalty should be awarded for both a deliberate or accidental handball. As it was, from the corner, Bamford bundled the ball over the line for his second goal of the game to give us a little breathing space. Harrison was in constant space down the right-hand side as Leeds kept attacking. Hernandez and Harrison both had shots saved to prevent us getting a third goal and Casilla made a further save to keep a clean sheet. It hadn't been a pretty game, but I was happy to get the win and three points. It doesn't matter how Leeds win as long as it goes in our favour.

Our next game is on Wednesday against Brentford, which sees Pontus return with the opposition team. Sorry Pontus but you need to go home empty handed with no points please. I'm not sure why we're not playing on the Tuesday evening though which is our normal day for mid-week games. We then go to Stoke next Saturday for the Championship game before meeting them again a few days later for the Carabao Cup second round at Elland Road. The away ticket sell-outs have reared their head again, with loyal fans missing out on tickets. It can't be right that someone who hasn't missed a game since 2012, went on the pre-season tour to Australia, got a ticket for Salford then missed out on Stoke. The club must look after loyal fans and not take them for granted. I love our worldwide fan base and will always encourage our fans to come to games. Although it doesn't affect me being both a home-and-away season-ticket holder, I do care about other Leeds fans. See you on Wednesday – LUFC – Marching on Together!

LEEDS UNITED V BRENTFORD 21 AUGUST 2019 AT ELLAND ROAD

It's been great seeing the feedback from Leeds fans who have viewed the documentary . Thank you for all the positive comments for my cameo role in it, which are gratefully received. I know some fans don't want to watch it and I can quite understand that, but I found I really enjoyed it despite the painful and emotional scenes at the end. We'll just have to go one better this year Leeds, so automatic promotion is a must please. It was nice to meet Rik from the Netherlands in the Peacock before the game, who came to introduce himself to me having seen me in the documentary. Having seen both the Derby and West Brom wins at Elland Road last season, we agreed it would be third time lucky tonight with a win against Brentford. It was nice to chat to some of our Welsh Whites before the game too. We made sure we went into the ground in plenty of time as I'd been asked to get photos of one of our mascots tonight. I'd met my sister Erica and friends before the game, and I managed to find her in the East Stand with my camera. In the toilets in the ground I was just entering a cubicle when a voice shouted, 'Heidi, that's my lucky toilet.' Well obviously, being the superstitious person I am, I understood perfectly, did the honourable thing and chose another one to go in and let Victoria keep the luck going.

Team: Casilla, Alioski (Douglas injured), Cooper, White, Dallas, Hernandez, Bamford, Forshaw, Klich, Phillips and Harrison. Subs: Costa for Harrison (65) and Eddie Nketiah (on loan from Arsenal making his home debut) for Hernandez (77). Leeds won the game 1-0 with a goal from Nketiah (81). Attendance was 35,004, with approximately 300 Brentford fans. Because the opposition had brought very few fans, this was the first game that the West Stand area at the front of the away fans became a Leeds United fans' stand again. Getting more of our fans in the ground rather than having great empty spaces was a great initiative from the club.

Today would see the return of Pontus Jansson for his first game against us playing for the opposition. I was sad to see him leave Leeds because he was the one player who brought the fans and the team back together again and for that I am grateful. I can still see him in front of the Kop

when he got us all going for the first time and that interaction with the team can now be seen all the time. As the teams came out it was good to see the interaction with Jansson and the current Leeds team, which showed he was well thought of despite all the rumours that had been doing the rounds. The South Stand also sang 'you're Leeds and you know you are'. I for one didn't accept the disruptive influence character assassination on him and at the end there were hugs all round with him and the Leeds players, which were good to see. Good luck to him, although not against us please.

As the teams kicked off, it was very much evens for a while, with Leeds getting a few free kicks before Alioski found himself in the book for a foul. Although there weren't many chances for either team, it took Brentford to hit the post with Casilla beaten to bring the game to life in the 24th minute. Leeds went to the opposite end, with Klich striking a shot that brought a good save out of their keeper. Bamford then put a header over the bar after a great cross from Alioski before a second chance of a header that went past the wrong side of the post. Brentford brought a save out of Casilla just before the break as we went in on level terms. The first half had passed very quickly though, and it wasn't surprising that we had not found it easy to get past Brentford.

The second half saw Leeds up the tempo, getting a couple of corners in quick succession. Forshaw brought a save out of their keeper and, with him coming close to scoring in the last couple of games, I feel sure a goal would come soon. We had a lot of the Kop shouting for a handball in the area and a penalty, which didn't come. It will be interesting to see a replay as I didn't see it. Dallas ended up with a booking after running up to the referee calling for the penalty as his pleas fell on deaf ears. Costa came on as a sub with half an hour to go to replace Harrison. It was interesting to see the new rule in force, that any player being subbed had to go off the pitch at the nearest point. That to me looks a good thing as there is nothing more annoying than players wasting time by taking ages to get off the pitch. As Costa started to make an impact, Nketiah was brought on in place of Hernandez. As I hadn't been sure who was on the bench, I found I was impressed that we actually had some players on the bench who could make a difference. As it was, within five minutes Leeds took the lead after some great work by Costa on the left-hand side in front of us. As he passed the ball across to the middle of the goal, we were all cheering before Nketiah had even put it into the net. I can't remember the last time we had players on the bench who could make an impact and also put some speed into the attack, which were great to see and get us the reward of a goal. Leeds were quite comfortable on the ball and limited Brentford to any attacks. Although they were still a threat for the last minutes of the game, we were able to come out with the win to stay on top of the league with another three points.

Stoke City away on Saturday sees us visit the Bet365 stadium again, which wasn't a happy hunting ground for us last season. A friend of mine who supports them said we will get two wins in a week as we also play them at home next Tuesday in the second round of the Carabao Cup. As always, I never take anything for granted and will make my judgements by what I see on the pitch but am hopeful we will put on a better performance this time. As Bielsa tends not to make too many changes, I expect him to put the same team out, but we will see on the day. If we get to the ground early enough, I hope to head to the Power League pub next to the ground where away fans are welcome and also to see my friends.

As we headed to the steps of the Kop to go out, someone said is that Heidi Haigh, the Queen of the Kop? Thank you for the compliment and, although I was grateful for the praise, I'm sure that view will only be from a few fans. On getting back to the car, I put BBC Radio Leeds on but was dismayed to hear someone slagging Leeds fans off who had been having a go at Bamford. I thought they should focus on the whole ground continually singing his name rather than some individuals who made their feelings against him known. At the end of the day they are entitled to their opinion whether we agree with it or not. See you at Stoke, LUFC – Marching on Together!

STOKE CITY V LEEDS UNITED 24 AUGUST 2019 AT THE 365BET STADIUM

It was a beautiful sunny day when I left Halifax at 7.40am to head to Leeds for the coach. Our stop was in Leek today and it was good to chat to friends and have a laugh. Just before we left, we managed a Leeds United Supporters Club Fullerton Park branch photo and thank you to the ladies from Stoke who took it so I could be in the photo too. As we arrived at the ground 45 minutes before kick-off, I headed straight to the Power League, which was a few minutes' walk from the away end. I was going to meet Ian (my daughter's godfather) together with his brother Les and his wife. It's a long time since I've seen Les, who is a Stoke fan, but both lads came to watch me play football for charity in the 70s and made a flag saying Big H rules. Les already thought they'd lose today and on Tuesday, but I was more cautious. That said, I felt more confident this time that we wouldn't make the same mistakes as last year, especially as Bielsa will have watched everything very closely.

I managed a few photos on my way into the ground and had a couple of fans trying to recreate the Beatles on the zebra crossing. I had to get my flag out for the steward to check it and had some lads saying, 'Heidi what are you hiding in there, a couple of cans?' I took the banter in the good spirit it was meant. There was a great atmosphere under the stands as I made my way to the green aisle for my seat. I got to the front of the stand and then made my way over to the left-hand side to hang my flag up in the little space that was left. I hadn't realised that there were loads of flags at the opposite end in between both sets of supporters until the end of the game. Never mind, but sadly it meant I didn't get any photos of them.

Team: Casilla, Dallas, Berardi, Hernandez (captain, with Cooper out injured), Phillips, Forshaw, Klich, Bamford, White, Alioski and Harrison. Subs: Nketiah for Bamford (74), Costa for Hernandez (80) and Shackleton for Klich (85). Leeds won the game 3-0, with goals from Dallas (42), Alioski (50) and Bamford (66). Attendance was 24,090, with 2,913 Leeds fans.

The Leeds fans were in good voice as I took my place near the front of the stand behind the goal. At one point I realised the fella behind me was sat down so moved slightly into the aisle for a

while. Even though I was quite confident, I wasn't taking anything for granted and knew that Stoke would raise their game for us. Last year they had just got a new manager in, but this year they were rooted to the bottom of the table and on shaky ground. Stoke took the game to us for a while but Leeds were able to quell any attacks, with Casilla not being very busy, just involved with our players passing the ball to him. With some misplaced passes for a while from Dallas and Hernandez, I just thought they'd grow into the game and wasn't too worried. It was a case of, let Stoke have their ten minutes and then we'd take charge of the game. Just after that Klich's shot brought a save out of their keeper. Hernandez was very unlucky not to get on the scoresheet on 15 minutes when their keeper made a great save to keep him out and then caught the rebound with a deflected shot from Klich. We had a couple of near chances, although the half so far hadn't set the world alight. Ben White was playing really well in defence and was so cool, calm and collected when picking the ball up. A couple of times he waited for the Stoke player to come near him before dancing round them with ease. As some fans were heading downstairs for the break, Leeds attacking the far end showed some great movement, before Hernandez sent a great pass across to Dallas, who was clean through to hit the ball first time into the net. As the Leeds fans celebrated, fans in the aisle next to me tumbled down the terraces and all ended up in a tangle at the front of the stand. Just as they started to try and get up, loads of fans coming back from downstairs came hurtling down the terraces with loads landing on top of one another. Some of them looked in a bad way as eventually they were helped up. What I couldn't understand was why no stewards did a thing to help, plus they didn't even ask any first aiders to come to where we were? A girl was let out at the front as she'd hurt her fingers in the melee and eventually came back with an ice pack on them. Just before the whistle went Klich had another shot saved by their keeper as we went in 1-0 up at the break. I spoke to the lad who looked really badly injured to see if he needed to go to the first aid, but luckily he'd started coming round and was able to walk.

After catching up with a few fans downstairs, including another one of our injured fans who I'd tried to help up, I went back to my seat. The lad behind me had scratches along his back and a big hole in his t-shirt. The lads seem to have been very lucky to have got away without being seriously injured, thank goodness. Although Stoke started off with a rare attack, it didn't take long for Leeds to get a second goal. Bamford passed the ball across the goal for Alioski to fire home to put us further into the lead. Leeds were on top at this point as they continued to attack towards us, with Harrison's shot creeping past the wrong side of the post. We had some long-range shots that didn't come off before we got a third goal. Forshaw played a great ball into the area, where Alioski found his shot saved by their keeper, only for Bamford to follow up and put the rebound into the net. Leeds had been playing some lovely football with great footwork, and although Stoke brought a save out of Casilla, we continued to dominate the game. With both Klich and Forshaw denied goals with saves by their keeper, we ended the game with a 3-0 win and another three points to keep us on top of the league.

It had been a great day out and I'm sure our performance will make other teams around us sit up and take notice. Bielsa ball is great to see, despite whatever happens in the future, and I for one am enjoying watching our team play.

Tuesday sees us play Stoke again, but this time at Elland Road in the next round of the Carabao Cup. The team will be made up of our youngsters and give players who have not featured much in the Championship some game time. I am taking all three granddaughters to this one, and as I couldn't get all our seats together in the Kop, I will move from my seat to be with one of them. Thanks to everyone who wanted photos taken today and for all the positive comments about my blogs, books and my appearance in *Take us Home: Leeds United*, the documentary. As always, I appreciate your comments, which are gratefully received. Also, I'd like to say a big thank you to Harry and Martin, both Bradford Whites, for buying my books *Back to Reality, Leeds United 2017-18* and *Once a Leeds fan, always a Leeds fan*. Talking about books, my latest one is called *Marcelo Bielsa's Leeds United* which is based on my blog and last season. Despite the way it ended, this was our best season in a long while with some fantastic football on show. As usual I have included lots of photos of our fans and this will be available soon. If anyone is interested in buying one, please do not hesitate to contact me. See you on Tuesday, LUFC – Marching on Together!

LEEDS UNITED V STOKE CITY 27 AUGUST 2019
SECOND ROUND OF THE CARABAO CUP AT ELLAND ROAD

I'd like to say a big thank you to everyone who took the time to ask me how my husband and grandson are doing. My husband is recovering from cancer but making good progress, although still very tired, and I'm hoping to get him back to a game at Elland Road very soon. My grandson Freddie was taken back into neonatal intensive care again but has made improvements today, so we hope he is on the mend. He is showing some spirit by pulling his tubes out, which is a good sign. Also, it was nice to say hello to those people who introduced themselves to me today, asked about my books, mentioned the documentary or follow my blogs. As always, I appreciate your support. It was a poignant catch up with one of my Selby Whites' family on their first visit to Elland Road since his death.

I'd brought all three granddaughters to this game, with the special price of £1 each extra for their seats. Danielle my daughter was in our normal seats together with Hannah and Alexis whilst I went to the front of the stand with Laura. We had a good view though and luckily when it did rain it didn't reach us.

Team: Casilla, Berardi (captain), Phillips, McCalmont (making his first start), Davis, Nketiah, Costa, Mateusz Bogusz (making his debut), Douglas, Clarke and Shackleton. Subs: White for Shackleton (45), Harrison for Clarke (45) and Forshaw for McCalmont (45). Leeds drew 2-2 after 90 minutes with Nketiah (67) and Costa (81) getting Leeds back into the game after being 2-0 down. Leeds lost 5-4 on penalties, with Douglas, Phillips, Costa and Nketiah scoring. Attendance was 30,002, with 811 Stoke fans.

After our 3-0 win at Stoke last Saturday there were always going to be changes to the team, with some of our youngsters coming in. This was also the chance for Nketiah and Costa to get some game time, having been used as substitutes for the last couple of games. Stoke started the game on the attack and had a couple of chances before Leeds started to get into the game more. Shackleton sent over a great cross, which ended with Douglas's shot inches away from finding the top corner of the goal. Then Davis's header towards goal was deflected into their keeper's hands. We were so unlucky not to take the lead in the 25th minute when first Berardi won possession before Shackleton passed to Clarke. The resulting pass from Clarke saw Nketiah hit a stunning shot that hit the post and bounced out. That build-up deserved a goal. Leeds carried on attacking and then, against the run of play, Stoke scored their first goal from a corner before getting a second a few minutes later. As the Stoke fans celebrated, including Les, a friend of mine, it was hard for Leeds as we'd seen plenty of the ball, but obviously we needed to take our chances.

The second half saw a tale of two halves as Bielsa made a triple substitution to change the game. He was definitely not just having us turn up but wanted to make a positive impact. This had the desired effect as the Leeds fans urged their team on. Nketiah's cross was just too far for Harrison to get on the end of as we had a couple of good chances. Butland made a good save

from Bogusz's long-range shot as Leeds limited any Stoke attacks. Butland was then caught out as Nketiah ran at him as he prepared to kick the ball up field. His kick hit his own defender, which gave Nketiah the chance to run at goal, round Butland, before putting the ball into the net. I'd said if we got one goal we'd get another, as Leeds continued to attack, and with nine minutes left we got the equaliser. Davis's cross was met by Costa at the back post to head the ball home. In the second half the Leeds crowd were in uproar as Stoke tried their time-wasting tactics by going down and having the trainer come on a couple of times. When they tried to do it again, I wasn't the only one screaming at the referee to leave their player on the floor and ignore him. Eventually he did just that, which was good to see, as that was one thing last season that drove me nuts. With both teams coming close in the final minutes with six minutes of injury time to play, the scores were level as the whistle blew, meaning the tie went immediately to penalties. There is no longer any extra time first.

Stoke took the first penalty in front of the Kop and scored all five of theirs, including one from Butland, their keeper. I thought there was a new rule when he took one and expected Casilla to step up for our fifth, which went to Harrison instead. After Douglas, Costa, Phillips and Nketiah had been successful in scoring theirs, Leeds lost the tie on penalties after Harrison's effort hit the post. It was a shame, but despite the loss the crowd chanted his name. I wasn't too despondent as we'd put up a fight in the second half and made a game of it. That puts the Carabao Cup to bed for this season as Stoke progress to the next round.

Saturday sees us play Swansea at home before the international break is upon us once again. This will see a top-of-the-table clash and I'm looking forward to the game. See you then, LUFC – Marching on Together!

LEEDS UNITED V SWANSEA CITY 31 AUGUST 2019 AT ELLAND ROAD

After another stressful morning I could have well done without, it meant we didn't get to Elland Road until late. As soon as my granddaughter Laura was dropped off, along with my daughter Danielle, we headed straight into the ground as it was too late to go to the Peacock. As we were walking along Lowfields Road, this man passed us, pointed to me and said, 'You see that lady, she was in *Take Us Home*.' As we went to go in the turnstiles, we bumped into another of the documentary fans so had a quick chat with Zoe and her friend Bethany, who I met at the premiere event in the Trinity Centre. After a quick visit to the Kop bar, Laura and I went to the front of the Kop to see the team training. It was nice to see Martin Hywood (who has done a lot of fundraising for Muscular Dystrophy) together with his family so managed a quick chat before Trampas shouted me. As usual I had taken photos of some of the fans I'd chatted with before the game. I also took some of the team coming out before heading to my seat.

Team: Casilla, Cooper (back from injury), Dallas, Alioski, Hernandez, Phillips, Klich, Forshaw, White, Bamford and Harrison. Subs: Nketiah for Bamford (61), Costa for Klich (71) and Douglas for Alioski (83). Leeds lost the game 1-0 with a goal scored by Swansea in the 90th minute. Attendance was 34,935, with 1,418 Swansea fans.

Leeds could have taken an early lead when a Swansea player nearly scored an own goal intercepting a cross. Luckily for them their keeper managed to get back in time to stop the ball crossing the line. Alioski's shot went over the bar and with his next one the keeper made a good save. I said third time lucky. Unfortunately, that chance didn't happen. The referee was winding the Leeds crowd up as Swansea went down after every challenge, gaining a free kick. Admittedly some should have been given but others were just soft decisions. After some great play from Harrison, the ball came to Bamford in the middle of the area, but he was unable to get any power on the ball as their keeper gathered it up easily. That was a good chance as he was in a good position, but it was a shame he couldn't just hammer it into the net. Dallas impressed me in the early stages, and although Bamford had been unlucky with a couple of chances he was putting a lot of effort in on the pitch.

Despite Swansea getting lots of free kicks, we limited their actual chances, but from a free kick around the half hour mark they hit the side netting. They had another good chance just before half-time before Leeds were unlucky not to take the lead when Cooper's header bounced back off the crossbar. The first half had gone past quite quickly as the teams went in level at the break.

The game had already kicked off as we came back to our seats, with Swansea on the attack in front of the South Stand. Leeds continued to attack as Hernandez brought a save out of their keeper. Phillips was hurt after he landed heavily on his back after a foul. Although he kept going, he was limping for a while before eventually going down and needing treatment. He did carry on and played the rest of the game, although he was not 100 per cent. We were getting into the penalty area and Harrison brought a save out of their keeper before Costa did some neat footwork around their player on the left and, from his cross, Hernandez's shot went over the bar. Leeds were having lots of possession and I hadn't felt worried about Swansea at that moment in time. With ten minutes to go, Swansea had an attack but the header went over the bar. With another Leeds attack, Dallas's cross beat the keeper, but Nketiah's header at the far post went into the side netting. As it looked like the game was heading for a draw, Swansea were the ones who got the winner in the final minute of normal time when Leeds failed to clear the ball in the penalty area. With that, Leeds fans in the East and West Stands started streaming for the exits, which surprised me. There was still time left to salvage something from the game but maybe they knew something that I didn't? It was one of those games where we dominated possession again but couldn't get the ball into the net, which meant we rued those chances we did have. This was our first defeat in the Championship this season and meant Swansea took our place at the top of the league as Leeds slipped to third place. Leeds didn't deserve to lose but Swansea took their chance to get the points.

With the international break ahead of us once more, our next game is away at Barnsley with a 12.30pm kick-off. See you then, LUFC – Marching on Together!

CHAPTER 3 – SEPTEMBER 2019

BARNSLEY V LEEDS UNITED 15 SEPTEMBER 2019 AT OAKWELL

After yesterday's glorious weather I was surprised to see rain on a miserable day. Although chilly, the weather had improved by the time I got to Leeds at 8.10am for the coach that I thought went at 9.00am. It turned out to be a longer wait than I thought as we weren't leaving until 30 minutes after that. I'd like to say a big thank you to Barry for sorting me out with a Swansea programme as I'd forgotten that I was in it with my *Take Us Home* photo. After a pub stop at Junction 39 (I'd recommend the bacon sarnies), we arrived at the ground about 40 minutes before kick-off. Because last season I had taken the cautious route as to where we would end in the league as I didn't want to jeopardise things, this season I'm not. I'm going to have a positive mental attitude and forget my superstitions. Leeds United will go up as champions in our centenary year!

It was slow getting into the ground due to loads of fans arriving at the same time but also because everyone had to file in one by one so the sniffer dogs were able to check everyone. The lad in front of me patted the Labrador on the head and was told in no uncertain terms to leave the dog alone as it was working – oops. I then had to produce my fire certificate for my flag before going into the ground. I headed to the front behind the goal to put my flag there as usual, only to be told I had to move it. All the flags were to be put at the front of the left-hand corner of the away end. I realised after that it was to ensure there were no Leeds fans able to get within feet of the Barnsley fans as they have in the past. I also donated my last book *Back to Reality, Leeds United 2017-18* to Garforth White's charity events. As it was nearly kick-off I headed to my seat, which was higher up behind the goal but a decent view. With this being the first game after the international break, it was good to be back at the football.

Just before the game kicked off, the lad next to me showed me a selfie he had taken with Radrizzani. I then saw him standing next to the tunnel waiting for the players to come onto the field. Although I knew it was late and I might not see him, I headed back down to the front and right to the tunnel. I saw one of the documentary crew with him and caught his attention, asking Radrizzani to come over. He did and said, 'I will have to talk to you at another game, you are famous!' I didn't manage to get my photo with him this time but caught someone else on camera. I decided to wait there as we were allowed to stay until the teams came out then went back to my seat for the start.

Team: Casilla, Cooper, White, Phillips, Hernandez, Klich, Dallas, Shackleton, Bamford, Harrison and Alioski. Subs: Costa for Harrison (45), Nketiah for Bamford (70) and Berardi for Klich (90). Leeds won the game 2-0 with goals by Nketiah (84) and Klich (penalty 89). Attendance was 17,598 with 4,400 Leeds fans.

Leeds set off on the attack and a lovely move from Shackleton saw Bamford bearing down on goal on the right-hand side towards the home fans, but his shot was saved by their keeper. Barnsley

looked a strong side which had ex-Leeds players Mowatt, plus Wilks, Halme and Oduor, who were transferred from Leeds during the summer. Some of their players were giants, and playing to our strengths today along the floor was going to be vital. There was a lot of end-to-end play and we had to thank Casilla for making an excellent save from Wilks to prevent Barnsley taking an early lead. He was also called into action a couple more times with good saves. Leeds carried on attacking and if we lost the ball the players would fight to get it back. Although Barnsley were strong and threatening, I thought we shouldn't worry as they could be beaten. Dallas and Bamford were playing really well, and I can't believe the octopus that was all over Bamford was never penalised once, despite it all being so blatant! We had a great chance to score just before half-time, but Harrison's shot bounced back off the post, so we had to go in with no score at the break.

It was good chatting to fans at half-time and also taking photos and, as always, I appreciate the comments and support for my family. Ian had come from the Isle of Man for the game too and for once I remembered a name to mention!

The team set off on the attack as soon as the whistle blew, but Bamford's shot was easily saved by their keeper. Casilla made another great save to keep out a long-range Barnsley shot as the game stayed at a fast pace from end-to-end. We thought when Bamford scored after great work from Costa on the right that we'd gone into the lead, only for the linesman to flag offside. Some thought Costa was offside, but on getting home my husband said there had been nothing wrong with the goal. As Leeds continued to attack, we had another great move but the ball from the left

was hit hard across the goalmouth and Alioski's header went wide. Barnsley still weren't giving up as Wilks hit the side netting and Casilla made a couple more great saves to deny them a goal. Another attack for Barnsley saw the linesman put his flag up for offside. Before Bamford was subbed, I was disappointed to see the reaction of Halme when he rugby tackled him. Although I still thought Barnsley looked a strong side, I was adamant they could be beaten. When Klich's shot was deflected just wide, I'm not sure if it was this corner or another. I said, 'Come on Leeds get the ball in the net now so I can go and get my flag.' A few minutes later Phillips sent in a great free kick which saw Nketiah in a great position to volley the ball into the net in front of the Leeds fans. There were great scenes on the terraces then, with the celebrating Leeds hordes. That was my cue to go down to the front of the stand to retrieve my flag before the end of the game.

As I got to the front of the stand there was a Barnsley steward at the front going along the stand making gestures to the Leeds fans. As everyone started to get mad our steward Phil 'Thumbsup' Cresswell went over to him to stop him. With that he lashed out at Phil and that did it, mayhem ensued on the terraces with Leeds fans going mad. My camera was clicking away with all the action, but I'd no idea what I'd captured until I got home, but the steward was removed from the stadium. Damn right he was, and he should never be in a position to do that ever again as he was unprofessional and let his own personal judgements affect what he did. What I hadn't seen was that he'd just taken a Leeds fan out for celebrating our goal. Why I ask, is it a crime to celebrate,

especially when he didn't even go onto the pitch? The steward then came back really cocky and goading our fans.

As I stood to the left-hand side, Leeds won a penalty and Klich obliged to put the ball into the net to give us a two-goal lead at the death. With delirious scenes of the celebrating Leeds fans, I suddenly heard a commotion to the left of us in the side stand. Some Leeds fans had been sat in the seats all game at the front but must have celebrated our second goal when they got attacked. One lad with no shirt on was one of the culprits but some of the attacking was vicious. Together with a woman, they were both attacking a lad sat down for ages before anyone intervened. I'd like to know why they weren't both arrested instead of being let back in the stand. The rest of the stewards stood around that area and did nothing. It was only when loads of our stewards ran over that it all stopped. One lad gave the Leeds salute as he was taken out. With it all kicking off and fans standing in front of me, I hardly saw the closing minutes of the game. At the end, I saw one lad with a badly grazed forehead, and I thought he was kicked it was that bad. I'd seen someone post before the game that they were vicious in Barnsley, especially if you are found in their ends, and that had been seen today. Just think, my little grandson could have been born there recently as they had to transfer my daughter to Barnsley as there were no special cots in Halifax. I'm glad to say that he waited to get back to Halifax before making an appearance. As I went to get my flag, I managed to say hello to Aravind from India who had come to see Leeds again and he said that he'd seen me in the documentary.

The win saw Leeds go back to the top of the Championship and Swansea drop to second place as Forest beat them at home in the last minute. Our next game is the early kick-off at home to Derby next Saturday so see you then, LUFC – Marching on Together!

LEEDS V DERBY 21 SEPTEMBER 2019 AT ELLAND ROAD

With my husband attending his first game since his cancer treatment ended, we picked up an excited granddaughter Alexis to head to Elland Road. It was a beautiful day but was to be a challenging day for my husband to keep out of the sun! We headed to Billy's statue on arrival as I was meeting friends there and also looking out for the wreaths that were being left for WACCOE who died suddenly last week. He was a well-known Leeds fan on Twitter, and he travelled with the South Wales Whites. I managed to meet up with a group of his friends as they laid their wreath next to a couple of others, including one from my friend Susan and Bremner her dog. He was also given a good WACCOE chant on the terraces from the 54th minute. It was nice to chat to loads of our fans there and take photos before heading to the Peacock.

It was one of those days when loads of fans wanted to talk, and it took me 20 minutes to get out of the Peacock car park as I was talking that much. It was a good job my daughter Danielle had already gone into the ground with Alexis. It was nice to see some of our Norwegian fans who follow my blog and others, including someone I used to work with. Earlier, Shona had said that I

knew everybody. I said, 'I do know a lot of people,' and with that the next person who walked past us said, 'Hello Heidi,' so we all burst out laughing as she said, 'I told you so!'

I got into the ground and went straight to stand at the steps ready for the team to come out. Straight away I was targeted by a steward, so I said I always take my photos and go to my seat once we are ready for the start. With that he obviously went and spoke to another one who knew me as he came to see me. I know it's all down to health and safety, but it does get overpowering at times. I know they had a word with a woman who had to stand on her seat as she couldn't see. She refused to get down unless they made everyone else in front of her sit down so she could see. In the end they said if she fell she couldn't blame Leeds United, which is fair enough and she accepted that.

Team: Casilla, Cooper, White, Alioski, Phillips, Klich, Hernandez, Harrison, Bamford, Shackleton and Dallas. Subs: Costa for Harrison (58), Douglas for Hernandez (73) and Nketiah for Bamford (79). Attendance was 34,714, with 1,024 Derby fans. The game ended in a 1-1 draw with an own goal by Lowe giving Leeds a 1-0 lead in the 29th minute and Derby getting an equaliser in 90+2.

A packed Elland Road saw Leeds taking the game to Derby in the opening minutes and, although we came close, Derby were defending in numbers. There were a few blatant pushes into the back of our players that the referee let go, although with one we were in possession and attacking so he played on. A couple should not have been let go though and, with one, Bamford won a great header under pressure, only for the linesman in front of the Derby fans to put his

flag up as their player went down like a sack of spuds. It was won fair and square and should not have warranted the decision, especially as they were given the free kick. It was obvious there was nothing wrong with him and we'd been denied a great chance to score as Bamford was in plenty of space. I can't say I knew much about the Derby players on the pitch to be honest, as it's a case of out of sight out of mind for me. I only knew Keogh due to him being called ugly by the Leeds fans.

Leeds took the lead following a free kick from Phillips, Bamford hit the ball back across the goal only for Dallas's shot to be saved by their keeper. Luckily for us his save rebounded off their player to bounce back into the net for an own goal to put Leeds into the lead on the half-hour mark. Dallas was unlucky not to get onto the score sheet, with a great save from Roos the Derby keeper preventing one and another kicked off the line. Harrison brought another great save out of the keeper as Leeds kept the Derby attack to a minimum. The linesman had already put his flag up before Shackleton hit the ball into the net just before the break. Leeds had shown a lot of attacking football in the first half as we went into the break 1-0 up.

The second half saw Leeds unlucky not to get a second goal in the first few minutes as Bamford's shot rebounded off the post. As Leeds were still continuing the attacks, I was surprised to see Costa come on so early to replace Harrison, who I thought had played well. Although Costa was quick to win a corner it took a little while for him to get into the game for me, before swapping sides. Bamford brought a save out of their keeper again before winning Leeds a penalty with some determined attacking before being brought down. Klich went to take the penalty for the second

game in a row, only this time he put it wide of the post in a costly miss. That was the difference with being two goals up and putting some distance between the teams. I wasn't too worried that Douglas was brought on to replace Hernandez, but it became apparent very quickly that we had started defending deep, inviting Derby to attack us. When Casilla lost the ball, Phillips was able to clear the ball off the line, but in injury time Derby upped the tempo and ran at us, which ended with them equalising in stoppage time. That was a blow but not unexpected and as someone said afterwards it felt like a defeat. I do feel that the subs didn't work today and bringing on a defender when taking Hernandez off changed how we were playing as we resorted to playing deeper.

It has been said that Leeds find playing at home hard with the expectations of the fans. What I will say is once we started defending you could feel the atmosphere change and go quiet. It's times like this when we should become the 12th man, but the players are the ones who can make that happen. Battle and fight for every ball and it won't go quiet. We had so much possession again today and have to start taking our chances, although we were unlucky with the ball coming back off the post and being kicked off the line. The penalty miss proved costly in the end too. At the end of the game, I wasn't sure what happened as Phillips was clapping the fans left in the Kop; he went to the front and had words with someone but didn't look very pleased either. As Alexis and I got near to Billy's statue we could hear a commotion up ahead, so we went and stood near the statue out of the way. With that, loads of police came around the corner with what I can only describe as a small group of Derby fans. Why they were bringing them that way I've no idea, but it caused a lot of unrest amongst our fans in the vicinity.

Next week sees us head to Charlton with ex-Leeds player Lee Bowyer in charge. If we can't win them all, then go out and make sure we don't lose another game. See you then, LUFC – Marching on Together!

CHARLTON V LEEDS UNITED 28 SEPTEMBER 2019 AT THE VALLEY

Well it was nice to see Leeds United rattle other fans this week when Bielsa won FIFA's Fair Play Award for letting Aston Villa score last season. Whilst that is one time I disagreed with Bielsa as we had scored a legitimate goal, it was funny seeing the outrage on social media. It's a shame there wasn't the same sense of outrage on hearing that Derby County had wrecked the away dressing room last season at Elland Road as well as leaving a brown substance on the floor. But even after the whole outrage from Derby over #spygate last season, which they whipped up in the media, they certainly haven't experienced the same outrage that happens when there is an incident related to Leeds United. After the drunken antics and car crashes a couple of days ago involving their players, they seem to have a lot less coverage than they should. Those in glass houses shouldn't throw stones.

As I left home this morning, I put my big coat on as it was raining and cold. Then someone tweeted me back saying it was warm in London, and I was glad to find out later that was indeed the case. We had a good trip down to London but hit road closures in the capital, which meant we only had just over an hour at our stop near Tower Bridge. The traffic issues didn't end there though

because it took us an hour and 40 minutes to get to the ground. Our coach had to park outside the ground itself, but the amount of time it took the police to decide we could go through after all was ludicrous. Whilst we were waiting for the decision to be made, a reversing police van nearly ran some fans over twice as he clearly wasn't watching behind him.

With 20 minutes until kick-off we managed to tie my flag up before my daughter Danielle went to the front of the stand, whilst I had to go around the stand to get to the top part. As the team came out, I found I wasn't feeling well, got really hot and felt ready to pass out. As my new glasses made me feel very dizzy, I decided to do without today and try them again another day.

Team: Casilla, Cooper, Alioski, Dallas, Phillips, Costa (his first league start as Hernandez was out injured), Bamford, Shackleton, Klich, Harrison and White. Subs: Nketiah for Alioski (45), Forshaw for Shackleton (45) and Roberts for Bamford (68). Attendance was 21,808, with 3,179 Leeds fans. Leeds lost the game 1-0 with Charlton's manager, ex-Leeds player Lee Bowyer, gaining the advantage over Bielsa. Once again Leeds were without a mascot and I can't understand why.

Leeds started on the attack, but the resulting corners didn't end up in the net, although their keeper made a save from White. We were seeing plenty of the ball but Charlton, looking a strong side having gained promotion at the end of last season, blocked most of the chances. We got another couple of shots on target, but their keeper saved the shots. Although we had been having most of the chances, Charlton won a few free kicks and on the half-hour mark they got the ball into the net in front of the Leeds fans to put them into the lead. That was the cue for me to stop feeling sorry for myself as I gradually started to feel better. Casilla looked to be at fault for their goal as I watched the replay on the screen. He looked to have stopped the ball and then let it trickle over the line. I'd said before the game that I thought he had been doing better recently, especially as last season it ended with me shouting expletives at him. I should have kept my big mouth shut again! Before I knew it, the half-time whistle had gone in what had been a fast first half.

The second half saw Bielsa make two changes with both Nketiah and Forshaw coming on in place of Alioski and Shackleton. Unfortunately, things didn't get any better as the terraces full of Leeds fans became quieter, although the home fans who were in good voice were helped by a drum! When Bamford lashed out and fouled one of their players, I immediately thought he was in trouble, especially when one of the Charlton players came across and pushed him violently. They both received a booking and shortly after that Bamford was subbed, which wasn't a surprise. A few players were letting their frustrations show today, including Phillips, which surprised me. Roberts coming on as sub upped the tempo amongst the Leeds players, but we weren't clinical enough in front of goal. Even though we had five minutes of injury time, we couldn't get an equaliser and ended up with our first away defeat of the season.

Lee Bowyer came over to clap the Leeds fans at the end of the game and did the Leeds salute. I'd seen someone mention the court case he'd been involved in and said that he'd not forgiven him for leaving Leeds. If Ridsdale had fined him in the first place I think that would have been accepted. To have Bowyer play out of his skin in those games during the trial, get found not guilty and then decide to fine him was wrong in my eyes. It knocked the stuffing out of Bowyer and the relationship with the chairman ended there and then. Things shouldn't have happened in the first place and started our downfall, but they could have been rescued if it hadn't been for Ridsdale, in my opinion.

Today was a bad day at the office as we never looked like scoring. I had a poor view for the goal in front of the Leeds fans so I'm not sure how close we came to scoring. With a home game against West Brom on Tuesday and back to London for the Millwall game next week, it feels like normality has resumed. It was good to eventually get home at 11pm after heavy rain most of the way back. A miserable day on the pitch had a miserable ending, despite the weather staying fine whilst we were in London. Anyway, as we are gluttons for punishment, we'll be back again on Tuesday so see you there. LUFC – Marching on Together!

CHAPTER 4 – OCTOBER 2019

LEEDS UNITED V WEST BROMWICH ALBION (WBA) 1 OCTOBER 2019 AT ELLAND ROAD

I couldn't believe a couple of the stories coming out of Charlton last Saturday. Hearing the stewards saying they didn't know they had to deal with a guide dog (Rita) on the terraces and asking if she would wee there was a good one. As Rita is a well-known Leeds fan, along with her owner Nikki, both of whom have gone all over the country, it makes me wonder where on earth they get these people from and where is any common sense. The same stewards refused to let Rita and Nikki, who is visually impaired, go out of the stand at the front to avoid the crowds at the end of the game. After a lot of arguments, they eventually relented but it meant they got caught up in the crowds going back to the station. The good thing was they were looked after by both Leeds and Charlton fans, so well done to them. Another story I heard was that the Leeds fans behind my daughter started scrapping in the 80th minute. For what reason I have no idea, and although everything calmed down they were taken out of the stand. I know we were losing and never looked like scoring, but we shouldn't be fighting amongst ourselves. Although it was sad one of our fans who had a car crash on the way to the game didn't make it there and another one missed his flight, maybe us losing helped to ease the blow a little.

It was still raining as we set off for Elland Road, and it looked like another miserable night was ahead of us. Luckily by the time we got to the ground after getting stuck in traffic it had eased off. Because we were late it meant no trip to the Peacock tonight as I had to meet David who had kindly sorted our Preston parking out for us. After a quick visit to Billy's statue to meet up with my sister Erica and friends for a chat and to take some photos (I was on the receiving end of some tonight too), I headed into the ground. I decided not to go and stand at the steps straight away, especially as I got in early, so I went to the front of the Kop. After chatting to Zoe (one of my co-fans from *Take Us Home*) and her family, I stood with some more fans I knew until the team came out.

Team: Casilla, Cooper, Dallas, White, Alioski, Klich, Bamford, Costa, Harrison, Shackleton and Phillips. Subs: Berardi for Cooper (went off injured 34), Roberts for Shackleton (45) and Ayling for Roberts (74). Leeds won the game 1-0, with Alioski scoring the Leeds goal (38). Attendance was 34,648, with 981 WBA fans.

The game started off at a fast pace and Leeds came close to scoring in the first few minutes, with Klich's shot ending up at the wrong side of the post. WBA kept getting stuck into Leeds and a few tackles had the Leeds crowd howling at the referee when he played on. WBA then started to go down at every challenge, and for a while the referee was giving them everything, but Leeds kept on battling. I'd said earlier that as we were playing a top-of-the-table side, that we'd be okay, and normally after a loss like we suffered at Charlton Bielsa doesn't make many changes and gives the players a chance to put things right. The Leeds team were definitely playing better and as a team, even though they were up against a physical team. After Alioski got booked for a late challenge it was the turn for WBA to start getting bookings as the only way they were going to stop us was by fouling. There was a shout for handball in front of the South Stand and everyone was going mad when the referee said play on. With that, WBA counter-attacked and I was shouting at Leeds to get back as it reminded me of a goal WBA scored at The Hawthorns last season. This time, though, they didn't gain an advantage as Casilla made the save. Cooper had taken an earlier heavy challenge from behind but eventually was forced to go off after half an hour when he started limping. With that, Berardi came on to replace him, meaning we'd lost some of the little height we had at the back. Berardi soon showed he was up for the game though, as he battled to keep WBA out, and this also eased any fears. Within a few minutes Leeds took the lead, although the chance looked to have been missed when the ball crossed the penalty area. The ball eventually came back to Harrison, who passed the ball for Alioski to hit into the bottom corner to send the Leeds fans wild. WBA immediately came back on the attack, and as they broke into the penalty area they were denied once again by Casilla. Leeds were unlucky not to double their lead just before the break as their keeper made a double save from Bamford then Costa. It had been a good half, apart from all the physical challenges, including the one that had caused Cooper to go off.

When the teams came back out again, Casilla had changed from the blue kit to the orange kit. Twice the Leeds United bench were spoken to by the referee and it ended with, firstly, Corberan getting booked then Bielsa, due to too many coaches in the technical area. What a farce, especially when WBA's manager kept encroaching on the pitch, but although he was spoken to he wasn't booked.

The second half saw Leeds come close after some great work by Costa, before WBA had two shots off target. Costa again showed some great footwork, brought a good save out of their keeper and Klich's shot from the rebound was blocked. He also saved another shot from Harrison. Roberts coming on for his first start after injury, made some impressive runs and looked on fire. Leeds weren't having it all their own way though, but WBA were kept out by good defending and another save from Casilla. With 15 minutes to go, when Leeds had just been on the attack, Bielsa brought Ayling on to replace Roberts. We were all mystified to say the least and couldn't understand why. We thought in the end it must have been because he was just coming back from injury, but that took the sting out of the game for the next five minutes. Luckily, this time we weren't going to sit back and invite them to defend as we got going again after WBA had got the better of us after the last substitution. With the crowd urging Leeds on, they battled until the final whistle blew to win the game 1-0. Bamford got the man of the match and I must say in the second half he really was putting himself about, showing some aggression and not being pushed off the ball all the time. The whole team had put up a battling performance to return us to the top of the table. Things could change before we head to Millwall on Saturday for another London game and early set off. It was great to get the win tonight – See you on Saturday, LUFC – Marching on Together!

MILLWALL V LEEDS UNITED 5 OCTOBER 2019 AT THE DEN

Firstly, my latest book *Marcelo Bielsa's Leeds United* has gone to print and should be out in the next few weeks, just in time for Christmas presents for the Leeds fan in your life – or you! If anyone wants one, please let me know so I can make sure I have enough copies on me. It was also nice to receive a copy of the football magazine *StaanTribune*. Seeing my name in there after an interview I'd done last season was good to see, although because it wasn't in English I couldn't read it, oops!

When my alarm went off at the unearthly hour of 4.43am I thought, 'You stupid sod, you've set it too early.' It then dawned on me that it was right after all as we were leaving Leeds at 6.30am, 30 minutes earlier than last week. As I still had to travel into Leeds for the coach, I'd allowed plenty of time to get there. As it was, with very limited traffic on the roads, I arrived in plenty of time so headed to McDonalds. A workman asked me what the score would be and said if I got it right he'd buy me a breakfast next time. I told him that I didn't predict scores as I always get them wrong, but in response to his 2-1 to Leeds I went with a 2-0 win. There again, as long as Leeds get the win and three points I will be happy as I don't care how we do it. It was nice chatting to Phil and others from the Griffin branch before I left for the coach. As I left, the workman repeated he'd buy me a breakfast if the score was right. As usual I got the score wrong, hence why I don't normally predict them, and although the workman got it right it wasn't in our favour sadly.

After a stop in Bexley Heath in good company, with plenty of recuperation talking, we headed to the ground. It was quite a surprise to hear that we weren't having a rendezvous with the police on the common this year but would be making our own way in. As long as they have police outside the pub where we turn right to the ground there shouldn't be any concerns. As it was, once we hit the common my stomach churning began, even though we had no issues, even arriving at the ground before the turnstiles opened.

After putting my flag up at the back of the stand, it was nice chatting to fans and thank you for the comments about my blog. Also, thank you to Martin for buying my first book *Follow Me and Leeds United* as your support is greatly appreciated. I left my daughter Danielle chatting to fans downstairs whilst I went to get some photos of the team on the pitch. When I eventually re-joined her she thought I'd got lost! Before going back up into the stand, there were plenty of fans asking for their photos taken, which was good.

Team: Casilla, Berardi, White, Ayling, Dallas, Bamford, Harrison, Phillips, Alioski, Costa and Klich. Subs: Douglas for Costa (45), Nketiah for Bamford (62) and Roberts for Phillips (76). Leeds lost the game 2-1, with Alioski scoring the Leeds goal (46). Attendance was 16,311 with 2,221 Leeds fans.

With a baying crowd behind them, Millwall started on the attack, seemingly spurred on by their manager leaving. I'd tried to banish negative thoughts about their performance so far this season, because there was no doubt in my mind that they would raise their game as they were playing Leeds, as per usual. Although Dallas had two shots, neither were on target. The game turned on its head 15 minutes into the game when their player went down in the penalty area in front of us. After awarding a penalty, with Berardi given his marching orders, we were up against it when their player hit the ball into the net, with Casilla going the wrong way. The referee was being really harsh with Casilla, saying he had to go back and stay with his feet on the line. In the end he stepped back over the line to see if he'd be happy with that! Later, social media was in uproar when it showed their player appear to dive and Berardi not even touch him. As it all happened so quick, I thought I'd missed the actual challenge, but it was right in front of the referee so he had no excuses. He should have evened things up for us when Harrison had his leg taken from under him in the penalty area at the far end, only this time the referee ignored the plea! For the rest of the first half Leeds were up against it, having to regroup, but this half belonged to Millwall. We weren't really in it during the first half as Millwall kept attacking and Casilla was forced to make a save to keep them out. Just before half-time, though, catastrophe struck when Leeds were unable to clear the cross and they got their second goal. We looked down and out at that time and had an uphill battle on our hands.

As I went downstairs I met Danielle, and she said it had all been kicking off on the stairs. Apparently, the stewards and police were trying to target Leeds fans who had made gestures back at the Millwall fans and were trying to kick them out. With the Millwall fans being their normal

vile selves by making stabbing gestures, singing 'Galatasaray, where were you in Istanbul? Always look out for Turks carrying knives,' it was no wonder the Leeds fans had reacted to them. On the way to the ground I'd read about Millwall being abroad recently and it ended with one fan seriously stabbed, a few more stabbed and others beaten up and put in hospital. Why they think revelling in the deaths of our two lads when they were close to it happening to their own fans is beyond me. We had been standing outside the doors to the stand, which had been opened for smokers, when suddenly beer went flying as things started kicking off again. One man had just bought two full pints which were knocked out of his hands and straight over him, so he was dripping wet. Obviously he wasn't happy, especially as he'd just spent the money to get them in the first place.

We went back up into the stand just before the second half kicked off. Wasn't I glad we'd made that decision, because within 16 seconds Leeds had pulled a goal back through Alioski. Harrison had beaten his man on the left of us to cross the ball into the middle, where Alioski had loads of space to bang the ball into the net. The lads didn't celebrate though, as they got straight on with the game. Douglas had come on in place of Costa at the start of the second half to give us a bit more steel as he had been very lightweight and not up to battling in my opinion. Although Leeds kept attacking, Millwall also hadn't given up and came close, with Casilla called into action once again. As Millwall backed off we continued to attack, and I thought Leeds would get something out of the game then. I thought Phillips looked impressive at the back and it was a shame we'd been reduced to ten men. It was funny seeing Phillips and Ayling's arm signals to the Bench, who were all doing the same. Sadly, our finishing wasn't good enough to come close to scoring though. As Millwall continued with their time-wasting tactics, their keeper surpassed himself. He should have taken the goal kick in front of us but instead walked around the whole goal and then got back to the same place he started from. It took until the 80th minute for him to be booked. The worst thing was the linesman was watching the keeper do all this but just ignored it and the referee was walking back to the middle not even watching. There was even no added time for time wasting, which was a surprise. It may have made no difference to the score line, but time should definitely have been added. I was surprised to see Nketiah coming on as I wasn't sure a battling game was for him. He made a few good moves then didn't really get into the game for me. Once again, though, I feel that Bielsa's last substitution with 14 minutes to go was a big mistake. To take Phillips off when he'd been involved in so much of the play didn't make sense. Whether there were any injury worries or if it was tactical to bring Roberts on, it didn't work for me. All that did was give Millwall the impetus to put us back under constant pressure, which woke their crowd up again. We had the odd break away but not enough to really trouble Millwall as we never got to grips with the game after that, especially as Phillips had been the king pin at the back of the defence for me. For the majority of the second half we had had the upper hand and made Millwall defend. I'd have liked to have seen us keep that shape and attack until nearer the end of the game because we had more chance of a goal at that time but didn't look like scoring once the subs were made.

As I went to get my flag the final whistle blew, and Leeds had suffered their third defeat of the season, with London not being a happy hunting ground for us once again. I still don't like coming to this ground. The Ladies toilets were a disgrace, they wouldn't flush, the sinks only had cold water and as for the hand driers … what a waste of space they were as they wouldn't dry if I'd have stayed there for a month of Sundays!

The longer the trip home took, the more down and demoralised I felt. Our ten men had battled in the second half, but I felt the later substitutions impacted on our game and stopped our attacking. With people falling out left, right and centre, I couldn't wait to get back home after a long day of 18 hours and put this game behind us. I am glad we have got a break next week before our centenary home game against Birmingham. It is still early days so let's see what happens next. See you then – LUFC – Marching on Together!

LEEDS UNITED V BIRMINGHAM, 19 OCTOBER 2019 AT ELLAND ROAD – CENTENARY GAME

Happy birthday to Leeds United and also to the Leeds United Supporters Club, both 100 years old last Thursday, 17 October. I'm privileged to have seen the best team ever play under Don Revie with my hero Billy Bremner. During my 50+ years of following Leeds United I have made some fantastic friends amongst our support and long may it continue.

In a week of celebrations for Leeds United, I'm proud to report that my latest book *Marcelo Bielsa's Leeds United* has gone to the printers and will be out soon. Someone said, 'Will it be out for Christmas?' The answer is yes so please get thinking about presents for you or the Leeds fan in your life.

After seeing the 100-year celebrations start with the 100 legends evening last Thursday on the anniversary of the formation of Leeds United, I got very nostalgic. Unfortunately, I couldn't justify the cost after the year we have had as a family, but I really wish I'd gone and sod the cost. As it was, it was great seeing all the photos from the event, which would have been a great networking event had I been there. I couldn't go to Australia either so will have to remain jealous of those lucky enough to be there. Catching up with the players from my youth and the best team that I have been privileged to watch, I have so many shared memories and they were awe inspiring. Someone said before the game that I should have been invited to this event, which was really nice to hear so thank you.

As I left home at 9am to pick up my granddaughter Laura and daughter Dani in Rastrick, I was aiming to get to Elland Road for 10am for the opening of the street party. Because we didn't get there until 10.20am there were over 1,919 fans already there, so we didn't get a prize. Both Laura and I won some chocolates for taking penalties against Lucas the Kop Cat. Well, Laura scored four in succession, including one from a rebound. As I've been taking lessons from Leeds United players, my first penalty went sailing past the right-hand side of the goal through the gates

into the East Stand. For anyone on Facebook who has seen my attempt, at least it resulted in a good laugh with everyone, including me. The only time I have played football was for charity with Croda Canaries in the 70s as I prefer watching the game myself. The first time was against Goole Dockers and the second time was against nurses from Goole Hospital. Because I was lucky enough to borrow a team set of Leeds United kits through John in the Pools Office, I wore number four for my hero Billy. I can still hear one of the nurses shouting, 'Stop that Billy Bremner,' when I ran down the wing. I did miss a penalty that day too, hitting the crossbar, but in my defence there were 12 goalkeepers on the line.

It was nice to catch up with many of our fans today and a big thank you to Craig and Michelle for buying my book *Follow Me and Leeds United* and Mally for buying *The Sleeping Giant Awakens*. I always carry one each of my books with me so have them for fans who want to meet me at a game. As I've just written my sixth book, the bag is going to get even heavier. I'd like to say well done to Andrew Dalton my co-author of *The Good, The Bad and The Ugly of Leeds United* for his new book released on Thursday. With this being an *Official History of Leeds United*, to hear that one was presented to each of the legends makes it a very proud moment for him so well done Andrew.

Having seen we had a 91-year-old Leeds fan being a guest of the club today, it was nice to see our youngest member, just three weeks old, making her appearance at the game. Baby Charlotte emulated my own daughter of the same name, although she came to her first game at six days old, interestingly both going in the South Stand, although in 1991 the South Stand was the Family Stand.

I'm so glad we managed to catch up with Nikki and Rita her guide dog as this was Rita's last game as she is retiring. With a film crew following them around, I'm glad there is recognition for them both as Rita has been an ever-present influence with our fan base as she joins in with the celebrations by barking. She will be sorely missed but is going to a good new home, so enjoy your retirement Rita you deserve it. On hearing the West Wales Whites had managed to get to the game despite having broken down after leaving home at 5.30am, shows just what our fans do to get to games.

We got into the ground very early, although I nearly got stuck in the turnstile trying to get my bag through with me rather than lift it up. By heading straight to the front of the stand to take photos, I wanted to be in a prime spot to capture pictures of the flags in the South Stand. Some fans had permission to have flags on sticks, which had badges from the good old days and it was really good to see. The Leeds legends were also introduced to the fans before the game and were greeted with many songs about some of the players, which were lovely to hear. Fans in the North East, East Stand lower and the Cheese Wedge held up either white, blue or yellow sheets of paper to spell out 100. With fireworks welcoming the teams onto the pitch, it was great to see Leeds United wearing tracksuit tops with their names on and then wave to the crowd. This resonated with many Leeds fans of the great Revie side, the greatest team ever. It was lovely seeing Leeds playing in an all-white strip today, with Casilla our keeper wearing green, another throwback to the late 60s/70s. Talking about tracksuit tops, it was great meeting up with the Cocker family today. Les Cocker worked alongside Don Revie and was an important member of his backroom staff. Les's son Dave

had brought along his dad's tracksuit top from the 1973 FA Cup Final. It was to be a special day for him, with his son Lee and grandson Cayne, because the young lad was going to wear the top at the game today. I had the privilege of getting my photo taken with it before the game too and Dave and his family are rightly proud of Les's contribution to Leeds United, and so am I.

Team: Casilla, Ayling, Berardi, Dallas, White, Ayling, Costa, Bamford, Harrison, Klich and Phillips. Subs: Nketiah for Bamford (45), Roberts for Klich (61) and Douglas for Costa (84). Leeds won the game 1-0, with Phillips scoring the only goal of the game (65). Attendance was 35,731, with 1,996 Birmingham fans.

There was a good atmosphere amongst the crowd as the game set off at a blistering pace, with Leeds starting on the attack and winning a few corners in succession. Alioski brought a save out of their keeper as we took the game to Birmingham. We were seeing a lot of the ball and continued to attack, although we lacked the killer touch to stick the ball into the net. Birmingham saw very few attacks until the half-hour mark and my fleeting thoughts were don't let them score against the run of play, but their shot went wide. Things quietened on the terraces just before the break as Leeds had a couple of good attacks. After some great play between Bamford and Costa, which saw the latter's shot blocked, Klich and Dallas were thwarted by their keeper as we went into the break on equal terms.

The second half saw Nketiah come on to replace Bamford as Bielsa tried to change things around. As we attacked the Kop end, Birmingham fouled our player before Nketiah was brought down in

the area. Instead of awarding a penalty, the ball was brought back to the edge of the penalty area to give Leeds a free kick. Sadly, the resulting free kick was sent wide by Alioski. The second half saw Birmingham start to come into the game more with one shot inches away from the top of the goal, before White made a brilliant tackle to prevent them scoring. With Birmingham starting to run at our goal down the centre of the pitch and shooting from the edge of the area, I said that is something we should still do. With our patient build-ups and passing the ball to the sides, we should catch them unawares by doing the unexpected. Roberts came on for Klich, which saw Costa up his game for me. A few minutes later, after good work from Harrison, the ball came to Phillips in the middle of the penalty area, who slammed the ball into the back of the net to put us into the lead. It was a relief in one sense as it stopped the crowd getting too restless. Harrison brought a save out of their keeper as Leeds limited Birmingham attacks. There was no way we could lose this game today, as we had to win our centenary game for me, and Birmingham had their keeper to thank as he prevented Leeds taking a bigger lead. Just before the end of the game in injury time, Birmingham won a free kick on the edge of the box in front of the South Stand. It was good to see the ball blocked and Birmingham kept out. With the clock ticking down, it was not good seeing the ball kept in the South Stand as adding more minutes on for time wasting was counter-productive, in my opinion. Luckily for us we got the win in our centenary game and the three points, as Leeds fans cheered when the final whistle blew.

We decided to head to the front of the stand as strands of blue and gold tinsel were fired into the air. I thought it would be nice to get hold of some souvenirs. As we got down the stand it

started kicking off in the West Stand with the away fans in the corner next to ours, in the South Stand. With police fighting them back, I was surprised to see their fans kicking off. Were they bad losers? I'm not sure what started them behaving like idiots, but this went on for ages before things died down. As we headed to the exits someone said they had let the Birmingham fans straight out and things were kicking off outside. Luckily for us the trouble was at the far end of Elland Road to where we were parked so were able to keep out of the way. One lad we knew hadn't been so lucky in the ground. Being at the front of the South Stand, he decided to get out of the way as he'd got his young son with him. As he turned away, he was hit in the face by a coin thrown from the Birmingham fans which put a dampener on the day.

With another game on Tuesday, our visit to Preston, before another away game at Sheffield Wednesday next week, it's going to be a busy week for football. I'm hoping I've recovered from the dreadful lurgy that started this morning and culminated in a lost voice, sore throat and upper respiratory issues. We will be driving to Preston so won't get there until late, but I'm hoping that my ticket will be fine. Luckily when my puppy chewed my ticket up, she left the bar code intact and most of the ticket so fingers crossed I can get straight in. See you there, LUFC – Marching on Together!

PRESTON V LEEDS UNITED 22 OCTOBER 2019 AT DEEPDALE

My little grandson Freddie went to the pumpkin place near Pontefract and met Stuart Dallas at the weekend, so thank you for the photo you had taken with him. Tomorrow night sees the opening event of the Leeds United Memorabilia Exhibition organised by the Leeds United Supporters Trust, so I'm looking forward to seeing what is there. My flag didn't make an appearance at the game tonight due to it being part of the Exhibition, along with my collection of badges, with most collected during the 70s. There was a little shop in the market that we always made a beeline for before home and away games (unless we set off too early) and whenever there was a new badge available it had to be bought. I'm very proud of my collection and my grateful thanks go to my late father-in-law who framed them for me.

My daughter Danielle was driving me to this game as we were both going straight from work. We encountered heavy traffic around Birch Services where we had a short break before arriving at our parking spot in Preston in good time. Having a pre-booked spot not far from the ground is great as we were at the ground before we knew it, but also before the turnstiles had even opened. I got in without any issues despite my puppy eating some of my ticket!

With my delivery of books only arriving today, I managed to get some copies of *Marcelo Bielsa's Leeds United* to take with me courtesy of my husband, who brought them to work. Glen was the first person to buy one, so thank you for your support. I'll have some at Sheffield Wednesday for those who asked for them and they are priced at £14.99 for those who wanted to know, so see you there.

Team: Casilla, Ayling, Berardi, White, Alioski, Harrison, Bamford, Klich, Costa, Phillips and Dallas, an unchanged team. Subs: A double substitution of Roberts for Berardi and Nketiah for Bamford (77). Leeds drew 1-1, with Nketiah getting our goal ten minutes after coming on (87) from a looping header that was helped into the goal by a deflection. Attendance was 18,275, with 5,648 Leeds fans, which as usual was a great attendance from Leeds fans, but I saw lots of new faces around. One thing I can't understand is why we haven't got a Leeds United mascot once again. With all the young kids who go to games it doesn't make sense to me.

Leeds won a corner in the opening stages of the game, but our chance on goal went wide. Leeds nearly gifted Preston an early goal with a short back pass to Casilla from Berardi, but luckily Casilla made an early move to win the ball. Leeds started winning corners and continued to attack the Preston goal at the far end, with Bamford's effort hitting the side netting. Although we had chances, we weren't getting any on target, which was frustrating some of the fans around me. The first half was going through the motions and Preston started to get into the game more and, with all the possession we had been having, I didn't want them to score against the run of play. With Alioski's shot going wide of the post after some great attacking football, we went into the break on even terms.

The second half started off well with Leeds on the attack, but we still didn't make the most of our chances and a lot of them went wide. Around the 60th minute their keeper saved one on target. With many fans getting frustrated and saying Bielsa needed to make changes, my thoughts were that I had to have confidence in his decisions and maybe we could turn things around. I know many were getting angry with Bamford as he couldn't get any of his chances on target, and whilst I understand their frustrations my take on it is that he needs someone with him, he cannot be the lone striker. When I think back, it took Chris Wood a long time to be able to take his chances when playing in that role. The one thing that Bamford has done is get more involved on the pitch, often playing on the wing, and he does a lot of work in that way that has to be taken into account.

As it was, Preston took their rare chance by running down the right and crossed to the middle when our attack broke down and were able to score with 15 minutes left on the clock. Bielsa didn't make a change immediately, but then brought on a double substitution of Roberts and Nketiah for Berardi and Bamford respectively. A lot of fans were upset that Bamford was subbed because I think, like me, they would like to see both him and Eddie playing together. I was brought up on football played 4-4-2 and it is a formation I hanker after, having seen the best Leeds United team ever play under Don Revie with my hero Billy Bremner. Now I don't know how I would change the team around in that respect, especially as they are brought up to play a different style of football. It may not be quite so easy to change things, but at times I would like to see that given a go. The same as last week, Roberts coming on raised the tempo of the game for me. We got the equaliser out of the blue, Nketiah headed the ball, which looped towards the goal then dropped onto the goal line. This was then given a helping hand by their player trying to head it off the line but only succeeding in heading it further into the goal. The drama didn't end there, Leeds fans were screaming for a penalty in the last minutes when Roberts was brought down in the penalty area. Personally, I didn't think it was a clear-cut penalty as I thought Roberts dragged his leg behind him, but it wasn't given anyway. Preston came close to scoring in the final minutes before the whistle went.

The positives are that we got a point away from home where Preston are undefeated this season. There are many fans saying Bielsa is stubborn, but I do think he has to go with his own judgements and not swap and change because someone says this and someone else says that. He does make little changes to his starting teams and it should be that players have to fight for places and not become complacent, thinking they have a guaranteed place in the team. Bielsa is very thorough in what he does and, yes, he will make mistakes as he is only human, but I still value what he has brought to Leeds United and our team as a whole. There is a long way to go until the end of the season and whilst not playing brilliantly we are up there at the top of the league. Personally, I am not a lover of expensive loans and would much rather have kept our personnel, using our youngsters as well as bringing the few extra players in. If we do go up, you will lose your loans and the nucleus of your team depth rather than keeping consistency within the team. That said, the one loan I do love is Ben White as he has done fantastic and fitted in so well, he is one player I'd love to keep.

A man standing in front of me said he reads my blogs and likes them because I am really nice to everyone, so thank you for the comments which are appreciated. Just as we were leaving our parking spot, the lady who owned the house came out and said we were welcome back anytime, which was nice to hear. I'd also like to say a big thank you to David Hill once again for his help in sorting this out for me.

We got stuck in traffic near Rochdale as the M62 went down to one lane but luckily got past it all after 15 minutes. It should have been shut altogether at 9pm but it looked like they'd kept it open until later (11.15pm) to let the majority of the football traffic from Preston get past first, which was good. It meant I didn't get home until 11.35pm, but still that wasn't too bad on the whole. Saturday sees the early kick-off and short trip over to Sheffield Wednesday so see you there – LUFC – Marching on Together!

SHEFFIELD WEDNESDAY V LEEDS UNITED 26 OCTOBER 2019 AT HILLSBOROUGH

Get yourself to the Merrion Centre this week if you can, to see the Leeds United Trust Centenary Exhibition with lots of fantastic Leeds United memorabilia on show lent by fans. It is well worth it and brings back so many memories. #LUFCTrust100 #100yearsofLeedsUnited.

I'd like to thank Adele and Harry from the Bradford Whites for their continuous support of buying my books. Today *Follow Me and Leeds United* and *Marcelo Bielsa's Leeds United* are the next ones they will read. David also purchased my new book, so I am looking forward to hearing feedback in due course. It was nice to meet up with Paul Wilson, the creator of 'The King of Elland Road' song that has been making its way onto the terraces. His music, along with photos from *Marcelo Bielsa's Leeds United*, have been put to video by Philip Daniel and my grateful thanks go to both of them for helping me get this out onto social media. Copy this link into your Facebook account to view the video, which I love watching and singing to:

https://www.facebook.com/philip.daniel.79827/videos/1207011026157348/UzpfSTEwMDAwMjY0NDM5MDU5NzoyMzg1MjgyMjQ4MjM2NTY1/

As I left home on a miserable wet day for Elland Road and encountered flooded roads on the way, I wondered if the game would get called off. With Hillsborough being known to flood before, it was always a possibility, but luckily, although raining when we arrived and the river next to the ground being fast flowing, it was still quite low down. We'd had a short pub stop at Junction 39 and got dropped off right outside the ground so got in relatively early. It was strange not having my flag to put up today, but as it's a replica of one I had in the 70s it was important it was part of the memorabilia on show at the Centenary Exhibition along with my metal badge collection. I had a few fans asking if we'd win today, but I hesitated as I said I wouldn't predict a score and just wanted three points. I'd seen Garry Monk mentioned in a few media posts, but it was only this morning that I realised he was now manager at Wednesday. That said, I knew he would make it awkward for us and it wouldn't be an easy game, although I'd have loved a replica of our 6-1 game here.

I went to the front of the stand to find David, who was in the lower seats, and caught up with one of our recent away mascots and his dad, who were also in that section. Last year there had been no issues with me going to the lower section to hang my flag up, but the Wednesday steward in charge today was having none of it. We were only having a quick chat, and although she relented for two seconds for us to finish our conversation the lad who'd let them up the stairs got into trouble. At least she was happy for another of the stewards to act as a go between though so at least

David got his book. I caught a poignant photo of Nikki, her husband and Rita her guide dog and I'm so glad I saw them. Last week saw Rita's last home game, but today was her last game with the Leeds fans as she retires as a guide dog. As soon as Rita heard me she started barking, which melted my heart and she will be sorely missed at games. Nikki will still be at games with her new guide dog, but I will look fondly at all the photos I have taken of Nikki and Rita over the years as she has been a fantastic Leeds fan.

Team: Casilla, Ayling, Berardi, White, Dallas, Alioski, Klich, Harrison, Costa, Phillips and Bamford. Subs: Nketiah for Bamford (went off injured 45) and Cooper for Costa (76). Attendance was 27,516 with 4,700 Leeds fans. The game ended in a goalless draw.

Within a couple of minutes, with Wednesday on the attack, Casilla raced out of his area but his clearance was a little haphazard, but luckily for us we got it away. We had White to thank for a great tackle as Wednesday were looking dangerous, plus Casilla made a great save to keep them out. With a couple of giants in their team who were proving difficult, Leeds were struggling to get some momentum going. Again, Leeds had plenty of possession but were unable to get that finishing ball into the net, passing out to the wings instead of having a shot many times. Catching the opposition unawares by hitting a first-time ball instead of that one touch too many could have made an impact and changed the game for us. The referee started surpassing himself (those fans before the game who had waved to him, please tell him he wasn't very good), giving Wednesday plenty of free kicks before Bamford had to have treatment for a kick on the back of his ankle. Casilla was called into action again just before the break before Leeds could have taken the lead at the death, only for Bamford's header to be denied a goal with a great save from their keeper. Despite the last-minute chance, it hadn't been a good half from a Leeds fan's perspective, and we were hoping for better things in the second half.

With Nketiah coming on in place of Bamford, who had been injured earlier, Leeds upped their game and we came close with a long-range shot from Phillips. Even with other attacks, we were still guilty of taking that one pass too many. When Wednesday ran straight at us attacking the far end and hit a fantastic shot straight over Casilla's head, I was convinced the ball was going straight into the net. Luckily for us the ball rebounded off the crossbar, hit Casilla, but then went wide. Nketiah brought a great save out of their keeper as he rounded their player in the penalty area. Leeds could have won the game in the last quarter when first Harrison saw his shot kicked off the line and then Alioski's header hit the post. In the final minutes Casilla made a save to give Leeds a point from the goalless game. One thing I noticed today was how bad Alioski had been when taking a throw-in during the second half. I was adamant they had all been foul throws, but it was only when he took the fourth one that he was pulled up for it. It was good to see Ben White get the man of the match from Sky though, so well done.

I'm glad we have a week off now before our next game at home to QPR, so I'll look forward to seeing you there, LUFC – Marching on Together!

CHAPTER 5 – NOVEMBER 2019

LEEDS UNITED V QPR 2 NOVEMBER 2019 AT ELLAND ROAD

I handed a copy of my new book *Marcelo Bielsa's Leeds United* to Stix, Leeds United's player liaison officer at the recent VIP event of the Leeds United Trust centenary exhibition. Last Monday Stix had been asked to call me to thank me for the book from Bielsa himself which was a great gesture. Imagine my surprise and amazement that had me buzzing when on Tuesday morning I received a telephone call from the great man himself. Wow, Marcelo Bielsa on the phone to me!!! For him to take the time to ring a Leeds United fan just shows to me what a treasure he is for the club. Although he needed his interpreter for some of the conversation and would need him to help read the book, he did say he would like to get a photo of me with the book. Hopefully, this can be arranged in the near future as it would be an honour for me. Fingers crossed this will happen. I would also like to thank my neighbour Keith for buying ten of the books at once.

Although it was another miserable day as the rain started again on our way to Leeds, my granddaughter Hannah and I headed to the players' entrance to see the team arriving. With the team arriving later than usual, we were there longer than I'd intended, which didn't work out well for some of my new books that were in a bag. Oh well, it means that my daughter has ended up with one of the damaged books now. I met up with Bev and Steve, our Bournemouth Whites, who did the foreword for the book as loyal Leeds fans, just as they were leaving the Peacock. Thanks for the support in buying a book and I appreciate their help. We stayed in the Peacock for a while and there was a great atmosphere in there and, with the weather being bad, it was rammed with fans. A young girl was attending her first game from Newcastle and I caught up with Mick from Nottingham. Butch from the White Rose branch was celebrating his 60th birthday and Chris, who stands behind us in the ground, was also enjoying birthday celebrations, so happy birthday to them both. I wondered why the Peacock had started emptying and assumed it was because the rain had stopped, only to have it pointed out to me by Hannah that there were only 20 minutes left until kick-off.

Team: Casilla, Ayling, Cooper, Dallas, Bamford, Harrison, Klich, Costa, Roberts, Phillips and White. Subs: Hernandez for Costa (77) and Davis for Harrison (84). Leeds won the game 2-0 with goals from Roberts (39) and Harrison (82). Attendance was 35,284, with 1,093 QPR fans.

The opening minutes saw some passes going astray as the wet conditions contributed to some scrappy play. QPR were seeing a lot of the ball courtesy of the referee, who kept blowing up for every challenge on them, which after numerous times started to rile the Leeds fans up. With some of them unjustified, it was good to see him letting things go more after about 20 minutes. They were also looking to waste as much time as possible. In the meantime, QPR had come close to opening the scoring but the shot went wide. Klich got into a glorious position in lots of space in the middle of the goal mouth but hit the ball over the bar. He looked to have the goal at his mercy, but it was only then that I realised how small their keeper was. Ayling headed over the bar from a free kick before it looked like Bamford had rounded their keeper and was going to slot the ball into the net, only for the ball to be whipped off his toes by a defender. With the ball ending up back with their keeper, he'd been so close to scoring. Leeds continued to attack and were stringing together some play down the left-hand side towards the South Stand but ended with Bamford's header going wide. Shortly after this, Leeds took a deserved lead when Harrison passed the ball across to Tyler Roberts who struck his first-time shot into the bottom left-hand corner of the goal. It was no more than Leeds deserved and it was good to get the goal just before the break. Although QPR came close to scoring when the ball was crossed across the box in front of us and their player missed it by inches, I wasn't unduly worried. Bamford had a header saved on the stroke of half-time before the whistle blew.

Although I'd been chatting below the stands with my friend Carole for what seemed ages, I couldn't believe it when I got back to my seat and found the Leeds team had come back out onto the pitch but not QPR. Leeds set off in the second half attacking the goal in front of us with first Costa, then Roberts involved, before the latter's pass just missed the foot of the outstretched Bamford. To me, Costa had been playing so much better today and, in my opinion, having Roberts there to help him made such a difference to his game. Roberts and Klich had shots at the goal before we got a second goal, or so we thought. Bamford's diving header after a great cross from Roberts had everyone cheering before realising the linesman had put his flag up for offside. After coming so close to scoring, it would have been great to see Bamford on the scoresheet, but it wasn't to be. Cooper had the ball and, as he ran towards the goal, some people around us shouted shoot. Well he did as they asked but it went wide, so they started saying you should have passed it instead! It was quite funny though. QPR had a couple of rare attacks before Leeds did indeed score a second goal. Harrison passed the ball across to Klich in the penalty area, but it rebounded back to him, so he slotted the ball into the net. Almost immediately Harrison came off as Davis came on and the young lad immediately ran at goal, but his shot was saved by the keeper. After another good run down the wing from Davis, the keeper saved a shot from Roberts before the whistle blew for full-time.

It was good to get a win and to score two goals to set us up for our second home game next weekend against Blackburn. Hopefully, I will catch up with a couple of fans from Australia and Mexico before the game. See you there, LUFC – Marching on Together!

LEEDS UNITED V BLACKBURN ROVERS 9 NOVEMBER 2019 AT ELLAND ROAD

It's been a busy week relating to Leeds United, starting with the opening of the Leeds United shop in the White Rose Centre last Sunday. I queued for ages with my granddaughter Hannah to go and meet the players who were there – Alioski and Meslier plus Josh Warrington too. We thought we were nearly at the front of the queue, only to find out we had to queue further in the unit opposite the shop. There was talk that the players were going at 12.00pm and we still hadn't got into the shop and there were still loads of fans behind us. Luckily they were still there by the time we got in and, despite being told we couldn't take any photos by a young girl, there were no issues when we got to the front of the queue, with Stix helping to take the photos.

Thursday saw the LUFC Trust, Allan Clarke and Paul Trevillion evening at the centenary exhibition in the Merrion Centre. With my friend Linda, who made my flag that is on show there, and my daughter Danielle, we had a great evening and the entertainment and stories from both Allan and Paul were first class. I could stay listening to them both forever. A well done to the LUFC Trust too for organising this, and also if you haven't visited the exhibition please go as it is well worth it. Allan said that to make sure Leeds fans have a voice, they should join the LUFC Trust.

Today I'd arranged to catch up with Daryll from Australia who had travelled over to the game last week. We'd been unable to meet up then due to the Peacock being so packed, so arranged to meet at Billy's statue instead. At least he has managed to see two home wins in a row! Sadly, I didn't see the lad from Mexico but hope he made the game. Thanks to Keith for buying my new book *Marcelo Bielsa's Leeds United* and it was nice talking to Tony about all of my books. It's nice to hear he will want to buy them all in due course, the same as Craig and Michelle who bought the new one today. As always, I appreciate all the support from fans together with comments made about my

books and blog. I do these things because of the Leeds United fans who are second to none. It was nice having a chat with the wife and daughter of one of the lads who I used to travel in to games with in the 70s who is sadly no longer with us. After going into the Peacock, my granddaughter Alexis and I headed into the ground early. As there was to be the customary minute's silence and last post played because today is the nearest game to Armistice Day in memory of fallen soldiers, I had to be there in good time. As it was, we got in early enough and I managed to get photos of the two Remembrance flags I saw on show, one up on level 4 belonging to Phil 'Thumbsup' Cresswell and the other from Harry, one of our Bradford Whites. I've got a photo with Harry that is in the latest book, holding the same flag up at West Bromwich Albion last season. A poignant day, but I've so much respect for those who served our country and it is good to see they will never be forgotten.

Team: Casilla, Cooper, White, Ayling, Dallas, Klich, Costa, Roberts, Bamford, Harrison and Phillips. Subs: Berardi for Cooper (injured 72), Hernandez for Costa (81) and Davis for Harrison (90+2). Leeds won the game 2-1 with Bamford scoring a penalty (30) and Harrison (35). Attendance was 35,567, with 973 Blackburn fans.

The game kicked off similarly to last week with passes going astray or not enough power in them to get to our players. With plenty of free kicks going Blackburn's way too, the one that really riled the Leeds fans up was being pulled back to the half-way line, where one of their players was down injured, when we were on the attack. Blackburn also started with some time-wasting tactics, but luckily after 20 minutes the referee curtailed some of the blowing up and played on. It was apparent to me that Harrison was up for the game today and on fire, with his speed down the wing welcomed. Roberts being back in the squad was also good to see and that has made an impact, in my opinion, which has benefitted a few others. As we started to get on top of our game, it was Robert's pass to Ayling in the box that resulted in a penalty given when the latter was brought down. The referee had no hesitation when pointing to the spot. Bamford got hold of the ball to take the penalty and I noticed he had a swagger about him that oozed confidence. Roberts went to try to get the ball to take the penalty but was told by others that Bamford was to take it. When Bamford put the ball into the net to put us into the lead, it took me back to listening to Sniffer on Thursday. He said he told someone the night before Wembley that he was going to score and Leeds were going to win the FA Cup, which they did in the centenary year. This game remains my favourite one of all time and seeing Billy Bremner presented with the FA Cup by Her Majesty the Queen was the highlight for me. The feelings were out of this world and that team is why I'm still the loyal Leeds fan I am today. Bamford enjoyed his celebrations and it will mean a lot to him getting on the scoresheet and should take the pressure off him. Within five minutes, he had received the ball at the left-hand side of the box, which he passed over to Harrison, who scored via the right-hand post to put us two up. I'd had no perceptions about the game or scoreline until then, but at that time I thought we could get more goals. As it was, Blackburn had a rare attack and won a corner. Kiko went for the ball but went straight back on to his line, only to see the ball headed past him into the net. I thought that was Kiko's ball all the way and he should have punched it out instead of waiting for the header on the line. It took the sting out of the game just before half-time, but we were still in the lead. With Leeds fans being in the bottom half of the West Stand because Blackburn didn't sell enough tickets, I thought we'd gone back in time. Seeing a steward making everyone sit down time after time, I thought how ridiculous. When fans in the South Stand, Kop and Cheese Wedge were all standing up it made a mockery of the decision.

As Costa got the ball in the second half, I said to the man next to me that I'd forgotten he was on the pitch. Although he'd been involved in some moves in the first half, they had been sporadic. With that, he started to get into the game more and looked impressive, with a couple of attacks down the wing. Obviously it is something he has to work on for future games, but it does show what he can do. With Harrison in good positions to receive the ball, one cross was inches away from Bamford's outstretched feet. Cooper had a shot saved by their keeper before he had to go off due to injury. I didn't see him go off the pitch, only Berardi coming on, so I had no idea what had happened. There again, Roberts had been brought down by his back foot, or so I thought. When I shouted at the referee for not giving us a free kick, the lad in front of me said he hadn't been touched. Well I know I'm biaised but I was convinced that's what I'd seen, but when things happen so fast it's not surprising that I see what I want to, lol. Harrison was my man of the match today, especially with the chances he had to score. Roberts was also playing well as he was fighting for

every ball and brought out a great save from their keeper. Blackburn had a rare attack but Leeds won the ball back and went straight on another attack towards us. When I thought the ball should have been passed to the left of us, it went straight down the centre, but as the ball ran kindly for us the final shot was wide. Roberts was brought down at the right-hand side of the box and the resulting free kick saw Bamford wacked off the ball too. A couple of times when Leeds were attacking, the linesman to the left of us made some baffling decisions. With the minutes running down, Leeds were able to keep the ball at the Kop end and win the game for another three points. I noticed that Roberts was limping after that last challenge so it's a good job we've got the international break next week. That was until I heard him say he'd been called up for Wales, so I just hope he manages to get over the injury quickly. I haven't heard anything more about Cooper's injury as yet, but hopefully that isn't a recurrence of the one he has just come back from and more of a precautionary substitution.

Next week I'm going to take advantage of the break to do some Christmas shopping before we return for two away games in a row, with first Luton and then Reading. Middlesbrough sees our next home game so hopefully I'll catch up with some of you then. See you there, LUFC – Marching on Together!

LUTON V LEEDS UNITED 23 NOVEMBER 2019 AT KENILWORTH ROAD

With the international break last week, I took the opportunity to spend some time with my daughter Emily and grandson Freddie. A visit to Elland Road was a must as well as having a photo taken at Billy's statue to meet my hero. I also received some great news during the week, when I found out that I will be meeting Marcelo Bielsa before the Boro game next week to have a photo taken with him and my new book. I'm so excited and what an honour to be able to meet him. With the book bought by Big Kev Wilky, who I bumped into in Halifax, and Nikki, who I assisted at the game today, my grateful thanks go to both of them for the support. It was also nice to hear that one lad had bought all my books and is waiting to get *Marcelo Bielsa's Leeds United*. I know this has been put on some fans' Christmas lists too, so I just wanted to remind fans that all my books will make great Christmas presents. Well done to the LUFC Trust, who have extended their exhibition in the Merrion Centre until Christmas, although only on weekends or when Leeds are playing. They have been able to get more things to exhibit and I was more than happy to let my things stay on display. I was also the lucky winner of a signed print from the 1972 FA Cup Final from the WACCOE forum draw and, due to Mark, I was able to get this today. Another prized Leeds possession for me.

After picking up Mark in Halifax, we headed to Leeds to pick Nikki up before heading to the ground. With a nice stop in Bedford we got to the ground 30 minutes before kick-off. As I was Nikki's carer today, after Danny's comment that I needed to bark, I had the coach in uproar when I asked him if he was calling me a dog? It was funny as we had a right laugh at the comment. It wasn't the first time I was told I had to bark today either. With Rita now retired and Annie still in training, Nikki is hoping that the Boro game will see Annie making an appearance with her at Elland Road. As we got in through the gates, the lad gave up trying to see what I had in my bags and let me through without even looking at our tickets.

Team: Casilla, Berardi, White, Dallas, Klich, Hernandez, Phillips, Roberts, Harrison, Bamford and Ayling. Subs: Cooper for Berardi (59), Costa for Harrison (65) and Clarke for Roberts (71). Leeds won the game 2-0 with Bamford getting a brace (51 and 90), although the winner was deemed to be an own goal by some. Attendance was 10,068, with 1,035 Leeds fans.

With the smallest allocation of away tickets this season, I hadn't realised that we had Luton fans in with us as I'd headed towards the no-man's land area. It was nice to see little Nathan from Halifax as our mascot today as he came out of the tunnel with Bamford. As there have been a few away games this season when we have not had a mascot, it was good to see today. As far as I could remember, it was also the first time this season that we have been turned around at the kick-off so Leeds were attacking our end.

The game set off at a fast pace, with both teams trying to attack. Although we didn't have many clear chances, we had a couple of opportunities where striking a first-time ball at the goal may have resulted in us taking the lead. Their player went down in the penalty area but I thought we took the ball cleanly as they shouted for a penalty. Bamford brought a save out of their keeper as Leeds had a lot of possession, before Luton won a corner. A fleeting thought I had was that I hoped they wouldn't get a goal against the run of play, which luckily for us didn't happen. A flurry of opportunities just after that saw Leeds unlucky not to take the lead when Bamford's shot came back off the post before, first Phillips, then Harrison, saw their keeper deny us the lead. Their keeper denied both Bamford and Roberts another scoring opportunity as we went in to the half-time break on even terms. With the rain pouring down, Leeds had played well on a tight pitch that just wasn't long enough for Harrison to get on the end of some of the passes. With it being an old school ground, we had to come through the houses to get onto the terraces. With talk of Luton moving grounds in the future, this will certainly be a relic of the past. I can remember going in the opposite end when Leeds fans were banned on some Luton season tickets and also we went straight to the game at Luton on our way back from Anderlecht during our European Cup run in 1975.

The second half saw Leeds attack the far end and their keeper once again made a save to keep us out. When Phillips won the ball from Izzy Brown, who was now playing for Luton, he went down looking for a foul but the referee said play on. White won the ball and sent a delightful cross for Bamford to run onto and stick the ball into the net to put us into the lead. We came close to a second goal before Luton had an attack. With Brown now on the left of us, he managed to get his cross in, which was headed into the net to equalise. With our lead lasting only three minutes, that was a disappointment. Their goal gave Luton the impetus to start attacking us and they had a couple of good runs when Casilla made an important save. With their next attack, the ball ended up in the net in front of us as my heart sank, only for the Leeds fans to start cheering as the linesman had his flag up for offside. What a relief. I was then very disappointed with the reaction of a Luton steward, who made the Leeds lad who was doing filming for the club move off the steps. He had been there all game and it looked to me like he was moved out of spite. We had a few more shots on target, which their keeper saved, but, with one shot, a bit more power behind it would have caused him problems. I suddenly realised that Luton, despite their early time wasting, would be happy with a draw as they hung back in the middle of the field. In that moment I thought that Leeds could go out and get the winner and should keep fighting until the final whistle blew. With the whole 90+ minutes of the game going really fast, Leeds had another attack and, as if in slow motion, Bamford's shot after Klich's pass crept into the left-hand side of the post. That was the cue for the Leeds fans to go wild, tumbling down the stairs, as I was trying to keep my feet and take some photos. When my toes were crushed by someone standing on my foot, I tried to move back across the front of the stand out of the way. Luton tried to attack us with one final push, but we were able to keep them out to gain the win and three points.

It was good to come away from the ground knowing we had got a winning goal in the final moments of the half. With another game at Reading and then Boro next Saturday, I will take each game as it comes. Go out and do your best Leeds and get as many points as possible whilst I keep an open mind. We can do it so just keep going. LUFC – Marching on Together!

READING V LEEDS UNITED 26 NOVEMBER AT THE MADEJSKI STADIUM

It was very disappointing to see all the empty seats in the home end today, especially since they have stopped giving our fans the whole end. With a 'singing end' that cost them money today, Reading is another club who are happy to throw money away, especially as Leeds would have sold more tickets for the game.

Team: Casilla, Ayling, Cooper, Bamford, Hernandez, Harrison, Klich, Phillips, Dallas, White and Roberts. Subs: Costa for Roberts (went off injured 34), Alioski for Klich (66) and Shackleton for Harrison (90). Leeds won the game 1-0 with a goal from Harrison (87). Attendance was 16,918, with 2,050 Leeds fans.

Leeds started the game on the attack but when this broke down Reading counter-attacked with Leeds chasing back in defence. Luckily for us, their player missed the ball and we were able to clear it. The game was fairly even, but Reading were keeping tight shackles on our players, resulting in some misplaced passes from us. Roberts went down injured around the half-hour mark and he ended up going straight down the tunnel. I hope it's as a precaution and not that his recent injury has flared up again, but this brought Costa on as his replacement. Casilla had to be on his toes a couple of times as he raced forward to get the ball in the penalty area then made a good save to deny Reading the lead. Leeds shouted for a handball incident just before the break, but the referee said to play on. I thought it looked blatant but would need to see it again to be sure.

Thank you Bob for buying my new book *Marcelo Bielsa's Leeds United*, having already bought some of my previous books. Another fan had just finished reading my joint book with Andrew Dalton, *The Good, The Bad and The Ugly of Leeds United*. As this book is based solely on the 80s, he said that it brought back so many memories of games he attended at the time. It is nice to get good feedback from fans too and, as always, the support is appreciated.

The second half saw Leeds attacking our end with some purpose. Again, the game was pretty even, with both sides cancelling each other out. With one attack, Dallas hit a great shot which came back off the crossbar in our best chance of the game. Reading were still looking for a goal themselves, winning a few corners, but Leeds were standing firm. With White once again showing great composure on the ball, I really hoped he would get on the scoresheet. When Alioski came on for Klich, it took a few minutes for the formation to take effect as Reading came at us again. Their keeper made a save from Dallas before Reading won a free kick just outside the area from another attack. After Casilla made the save, their player was stopped by Dallas from crossing it back into the area. Harrison picked the ball up as Leeds raced out of defence with a fantastic move, passed back to Dallas who, with a great cross-field ball, found Alioski haring down the wing. He then passed the ball to Costa, whose pin-point cross found Harrison at the far post in acres of space to head the ball into the net and send the Leeds fans wild behind the goal. Apparently, it took 15 seconds from defence to scoring the goal, with Harrison involved in both the start and finish of the

129

move – wow! Just before we scored, I felt we would fight until the end and there was always that chance of a late goal. Some Leeds fans must have been in the stand to the right because just after we scored loads of Reading fans and stewards went chasing down the tunnel. I'd seen some fans thrown out earlier in the game in the same area, but I wasn't sure if they were Leeds fans or not. It was good to see Shackleton back on the pitch, even if it was only for injury time. Leeds weren't going to let Reading get back into the game as we held on for the win and another three points to put us on top of the league. A very happy fan base left the ground to head home.

I'll be there early on Saturday as I've to be at the players' entrance by 1.15pm to get my photo taken with Marcelo Bielsa and my new book. I'm so excited, as is my granddaughter Hannah, and can't wait, so see you there. LUFC – Marching on Together!

LEEDS UNITED V MIDDLESBROUGH 30 NOVEMBER 2019 AT ELLAND ROAD

We headed into Leeds early today as I was meeting Marcelo Bielsa to have a photo taken with my new book *Marcelo Bielsa's Leeds United*. After dreaming half the night about trying to get to meet him but it not happening, I was happy to get to the ground in good time. After meeting Stix at the players' entrance, my husband, granddaughter Hannah and I were taken into the players' lounge to wait for the team and Bielsa to arrive. Nice and friendly staff in there contributed to a very welcoming atmosphere, so thank you for that. When Stix came to get me, I wasn't sure

what to expect as I thought I'd just get my photo taken at the entrance. As it was, I was taken into the manager's office where I got a big hug from Bielsa before going to face the cameras. I wasn't expecting to be filmed and, in the rush, I nearly forgot I wanted a photo with my book. The first photo saw Bielsa doing the Leeds salute with me too, then I got the other one. After getting a final hug from Bielsa and getting my book signed by him later as I'd forgotten to do that also, I'd like to say that he is a man in a million. Hannah said she wanted the signed book but, unfortunately for her, this one is mine to keep. She then asked if she could have it when I die. I had to laugh at that and said she may need to fight my daughter Danielle for it! Getting this opportunity today though was absolutely brilliant and I am grateful to Stix for arranging this for me – thank you to him too.

After a visit to the Peacock we got into the ground before the teams came out. As there had been a heavy frost this morning, I was expecting it to be colder but had wrapped up well. The sun had been shining, making it a nice day for a game of football. I said to a few people that Leeds would win 5-0 today. I know it was a tongue-in-cheek score line, but one day someone is going to get a hammering so why not start today? As it was, I was very close to being right, although my daughter thought I'd had a knock on the head, so to speak.

Team: Casilla, Ayling, Cooper, White, Dallas, Hernandez, Phillips, Costa, Bamford, Klich and Harrison. Subs: Costa for Alioski (76), Nketiah for Bamford (79) and Berardi for Phillips (83). Leeds won the game 4-0 with goals from Bamford (3), a brace from Klich (45+3 and 73) and Costa (67). Attendance was 35,626, with 1,806 Middlesbrough fans.

Leeds set off on the attack at a fast pace, which ended with Ayling's shot going wide of the post. As Leeds continued to attack, with Harrison running at the defence, their keeper pushed out the resulting header from Bamford. When the ball came back out to Hernandez on the right, his pass found Bamford again, only this time his header was put into the net to give Leeds an early lead after three minutes. Bamford was very unlucky not to get a second shortly afterwards, but he was denied again by their keeper. The pace of the game quietened down after approximately 20 minutes and, although Boro were seeing more of the ball, Leeds were able to deal with them. Some passing was short, which gave Boro a bit of hope when they won the ball back. When Casilla whipped the ball off the toes of one of the Boro players, leaving him on his backside, the Leeds fans cheered. It had been a close call, but he was very cool and all credit to him. As half-time approached, Bamford got the ball at the left-hand side of the penalty area. His cross came back to Klich, who then, with the luck of a deflection, put the ball into the net to double our lead. That was great timing just on the stroke of half-time.

The fans were in good voice at the start of the second half and the two-goal lead had given us some breathing space. We were unlucky not to get a further goal but that was thanks to their keeper making a good save from Harrison. When the fans shouted at Dallas to shoot, well he did as they asked, but unfortunately the resulting shot was well wide. We did indeed get another goal when Costa, after some good play, got into the penalty area and scored our third of the day. This was also his first league goal for Leeds. Casilla was called into action before the Leeds attack was seen at the Kop end again. When Leeds took a short corner, the ball came to Klich on the edge of the box to the right of us. He let fly with a great shot that ended up in the top left-hand side of the goal to us. Four goals on the day and I came close to the right score when Phillips's free kick nearly made it five, only for their keeper to once again make a great save to deny him a goal. Despite Boro seeing some of the ball, they didn't really pose a threat. I knew Woodgate, our ex-player, was managing them now, but I'd forgotten about Howson playing for them and only saw him clapping the fans at the end.

After finishing my blog tonight, it will be time to put up my Leeds United-coloured Christmas tree as it comes up to my favourite time of the year. I want a better ending than last year as it comes up to the first anniversary of my husband finding out he had cancer. We've had a very challenging year as a family, but we can at least look forward, not everyone can. With our grandson Freddie growing and now looking like a little baby not a preemie, he continues to make good progress.

Thank you to both Gary and Roy for buying my new book, I hope you enjoy the read. Today was a good result for us, making it five wins out of five, and takes us into our early kick-off next Saturday at Huddersfield. Unfortunately for us, Phillips will be banned for this one due to his booking today. I'll be driving to this one so see you there, LUFC – Marching on Together!

CHAPTER 6 – DECEMBER 2019

HUDDERSFIELD V LEEDS UNITED 7 DECEMBER 2019 AT THE JOHN SMITH'S STADIUM

First of all, with this day being the 22nd anniversary since the death of my hero Billy Bremner, my thoughts go out to his family. I can't believe it is so many years ago that I, along with thousands of other fans, lined the streets near Doncaster to say goodbye. My Bremner stone is near Billy's feet at Elland Road and it is something I am proud to own, courtesy of my family. Leeds fans in the crowd at Huddersfield paid their tributes to the great man by chanting Billy Bremner's barmy army over and over again.

I'd been talking to a couple of Huddersfield fans at work yesterday. One said that they wished they'd never been in the Premiership as they now have overpaid prima donnas who won't play (it looks like some were dropped for today too, which proves a point). After seeing the display from some of their players today, who went down at the drop of a hat, that is one thing I don't miss – give me our Leeds players any day.

With driving to the game today, it was great to meet my daughter Danielle at my elder daughter's house in Rastrick, because 15 minutes later we were parked up at the ground. The parking attendant thanked me for being so good and quick to park and said I could teach others

how to park properly. It's a good job he didn't see me trying to park on the roadside when I went to babysit my grandson later that evening, hence the late blog so apologies for that. We decided to wait for the Leeds coaches to arrive before we eventually went into the ground. As we headed up the hill to the car park as normal, it was only because of some other Leeds fans that we didn't have a wasted trip to the turnstiles. Huddersfield had changed where we entered the ground, so we entered just past where the coaches parked instead. I didn't have any issues with that and it was only after we turned around that stewards were told to stop any Leeds fans heading that way.

We got into the ground in good time and had a right laugh when Danielle was asked if she was old enough to be searched. As the age is 16 and she is well into her 20s, it looks like she is carrying on the family tradition of looking younger. Well my friend Sue and I have remained 35 for a number of years, so I forget my real age – lol! Thank you to the Bradford Whites for their support and promotion of my books for me. It was funny to hear Adele had been reading one of them whilst in a meeting recently and couldn't put it down as she got so engrossed in it. Well it was a lot more interesting wasn't it – lol? Thanks to Gary Noble for buying my new book *Marcelo Bielsa's Leeds United* too. Don't forget these books will make a great present for any Leeds fan.

It was nice to meet up with a steward who helped save a friend of mine's life at the Middlesbrough game last week. He saw Mags collapse near the LUDO lounge and realised she needed immediate help, despite the fact she had been drinking, as someone said. His quick response was to get her to the first aid bay, then the nurse and doctor in there had to give her CPR as her heart stopped three times. Well done to Martin Grubb, Catriona and Dr Paul Robinson because without them Mags wouldn't be here today.

Casilla had a couple of friends in the stand who had travelled from Italy for the game today. He made a couple of crucial saves which kept us in the game, so well done to him. He has come a long way since I was shouting expletives at him after the Derby game and I'll put my hands up to say that, now, I do feel safe with him in goal. His charging out of the area has been brought under control and that has made such a difference to the way he plays.

Just before we'd gone to our seats for the start of the game, we'd been standing outside the stairs next to the partition between the sets of fans. The Town fans started banging on the other side of the walls before deciding some of us needed a beer bath, so that was reciprocated very quickly. I made sure the stewards were told it had come our way first as well as a bottle, as it was straight away looking like our fans were about to get the blame. At half-time there were a number of police and stewards in the same place on our side.

Team: Casilla, Ayling, White, Berardi, Dallas, Harrison, Costa, Bamford, Klich, Alioski and Hernandez. Subs: Nketiah for Bamford (77), Oliver Casey making his first-team debut for Klich (85) and Douglas for Costa (87). Leeds won the game 2-0 with goals from Alioski (50) and Hernandez (78). Attendance was 23,805, with 2,314 Leeds fans.

I was looking forward to us winning today but knew it wouldn't be an easy game because Town were going to raise their game against us and there were no doubts in my mind that would be the case. It did prove to be a difficult game, but with Cooper being out through injury and Phillips suspended for this game, we had to reshuffle the squad at the back. It was apparent to me that White took a short while to settle in because of this, but it didn't take long for him to get there. The one thing Leeds were doing was chasing after every ball lost, and that proved to be a good thing many a time when we won the ball back. I was hoping our fitness would tell in the end though.

Town were given a few free kicks to begin with before things settled down slightly as they were going down at the drop of a hat. Two of their players did have a clash of heads, which was a justified stoppage. Leeds managed to get on the attack and won a corner. Hernandez sent a low cross into the box and Klich's shot bounced off the post and away for our first chance of the game. Town retaliated with an attack but found Casilla in great form as he made a fantastic save to keep them out. After one of their players had been down 'injured' for a while – more like time wasting to me – it didn't take him long to start running around in the penalty area. Leeds players were after them like flies and, with one of their players on the goal line, Alioski was being a right pest lol as they ran around Casilla. Alioski was doing his job and protecting his keeper! Leeds were standing firm, with Casilla making another save, and we nearly took the lead just before the break as we raced to the other end, but Costa's shot went over. I was glad that we'd got to half-time and kept Town out, especially as there had been five minutes of injury time played.

At half-time a lad had gone into the ladies' toilets causing uproar but had disappeared before the stewards arrived. It was nice to hear that a lad going through cancer treatment is responding well to it and good luck in his recovery. Another lad who I'd put in touch with my publisher is getting his book published in March, which was good to hear. After having my photo taken with Bielsa last week, that caused a good topic of conversation with others. I was talking to people that much and taking photos that I decided I better head back into the stand as I was sure the second half would have kicked off. That proved to be the case, but luckily I hadn't missed anything. I had only just got back to my seat as Leeds were on the attack and won a corner. The ball came to Alioski on the edge of the box, and as soon as the ball left his foot I knew it was a goal as the Leeds fans went wild. With the hatred from Town fans that never existed until we ended up in the same league, it just made me want to win even more, so get in! Trying to keep my feet when everyone was falling around me was difficult as I scraped my leg on the seat in front. Just after that we had another great attack, only Bamford's final header was wide. That was a shame as we could have put the game to bed then. When Bamford did score, his goal was ruled out for offside, but replays apparently showed that the goal should have stood. Their keeper saved from Harrison, which kept them in the game. Two of our players were booked – Klich and White – when both of them won the ball, from what I could see. Hopefully, I'll get to see these again, as the ball went in the right direction after the tackle. Although Town players kept going down, it was noticeable that they

didn't stay down as long now they were behind. When it looked like Town had got the better of our defence and were going to equalise, Casilla made a point-blank save with his feet, which enabled us to bring the ball out of defence. Leeds were starting to make some breaks now and Bamford was starting to get under their skins with a foul eventually bringing him down. Even though he had hurt his arm, our trainers did not come onto the pitch and he eventually got up and carried on. This angered their fans too – haha. Eventually Bamford got subbed for Nketiah and, as he went off, he put his thumbs up to the dugout, job done! Within a minute Leeds took a greater lead with a second goal, after breaking away with another fantastic move which ended with Hernandez heading the ball into the net in front of the Leeds fans. Delirious scenes on the terraces as the lads behind me tumbled down the seats, and I couldn't keep my footing and ended up on the floor too. Eventually we all got up and I managed a few photos with lots of happy Leeds fans. That's all part of the football experience, although different from falling down the terraces in the past with no seats. The lad did ask if I was OK, which was nice. For those saying safe standing isn't required, with railings in place it would certainly stop people falling over lots of seats onto others. With the early kick-off result, Leeds had gone back to the top of the table again. As the Leeds fans continued to sing and celebrate, the Town fans started to leave the stadium in abundance knowing they had been beaten. At the end of the game it was nice to see some of the Leeds players interacting with some Town players and Alioski swapped shirts.

We were some of the last Leeds fans to leave the stadium as we were near the front of the stand. As we walked past the Leeds coaches, I started taking photos of some of our fans, but it looked like I was causing a riot. Well a friendly one, lol. As we got to the crossroads by the Ford garage, I saw some of the walkers from the Leeds United Trust. They had walked to the ground today from Elland Road with some Town fans to raise money for the foodbanks, so well done to them. As we stood there, loads of police came running past us and vans shot up the road towards the town centre. To say it was so long after the game, I can only surmise that our stragglers had been met by some Town fans, but no doubt someone will say what happened in time.

Well done Leeds, another three points and onto our midweek game at home to Hull on Tuesday. Keep going and let's enjoy what we are seeing, see you there, LUFC – Marching on Together!

LEEDS UNITED V HULL CITY 10 DECEMBER 2019 AT ELLAND ROAD

As I left Rastrick with my granddaughter Alexis, the heavens opened into monsoon weather. I wasn't looking forward to the journey to Elland Road, or the thought of being outside in it. As it was, I didn't have any reason to worry because severe traffic issues at a standstill both on the motorway and around the ground ensured we didn't get to the game until after kick-off. That was probably caused by bad judgement on my part as I thought it would be easier to get Alexis her McDonalds at the White Rose Centre. Well that part was fine, and it was nice to bump into one of our Welsh Whites who said his journey over the tops had been horrendous. Leaving the White

Rose saw a 45-minute journey to our parking spot at Elland Road, so by the time we got in the ground the game had kicked off. Luckily, we hadn't missed anything, although I didn't get my customary photos of the team coming out with the mascots so apologies to those who like seeing them. We did miss the cat on the pitch that had to be removed from the ground.

Team: Casilla, Ayling, Berardi, Phillips (back from suspension), Hernandez, Bamford, Klich, Harrison, Costa, White and Dallas. Subs: Alioski for Harrison (69), Struijk (making his debut) for Costa (91) and Douglas for Klich (96). Leeds won 2-0 with an own goal from De Wijs (73) and Alioski scoring the second (82). Attendance was 35,200, with 1,512 Hull fans.

It took me another ten minutes before there was enough break in play to get my glasses out. Although Leeds were seeing a lot of the ball, some of our passing wasn't always on target. That said, Hull were making it difficult for us with some tight marking, which we got around with some lovely touches. Hernandez was denied a goal by their keeper after a great one-two with Costa had put him in a great position to get the shot in. When Hull had a shot from the corner that hit the side netting, their fans thought they had scored. The Leeds fans retaliated with some gallows humour, cheering and pretending to score a goal. At the other end Leeds came close when Berardi got on the end of a Phillips' corner and put the shot narrowly wide. Although Leeds had a few more shots, none were on target.

It was only at the start of the second half that I realised Hull had turned us around at the start of the game. Very observant! Hull were still marking us tightly, leaving it a slightly frustrating game, not helped by the referee at times. Hull were getting into the game more and trying to attack, having a couple of shots, and at that point I thought we should change things. As it was, Bielsa thought differently and as usual I trusted his judgement. The ground had gone silent again and I said we needed to up the singing so as not to affect the players. As the crowd started getting behind them, Costa found his goal chalked off due to offside. I'd seen the flag go up straight away before he put the ball into the net, which was a shame. I said, 'Right Leeds, we'd better score again then.' One of their players did a blatant dive in the penalty area right in front of us, trying to get a penalty, and he got plenty of boos for his effort. One of their attackers looked out of breath and I was sure that our fitness levels would get the better of them in the end, although at that time it looked like a goalless draw was on the cards. Hull had been making things difficult for us to get any flow to our play going. With our next attack, we did indeed get a goal, courtesy of an own goal from a Hull player after Costa's cross wrong-footed their keeper. I wasn't worried about any of Hull's attacks after we went in front as our players were backing each other up and fighting for the ball. I thought Ayling and Berardi had played exceptionally well and made some important tackles. Alioski came on as sub and a few minutes later Casilla made a fantastic save with the help of Bamford to keep Hull out. With that, Leeds raced to the South Stand down the right-hand side of the pitch. Klich passed the ball to Bamford in the middle and unfortunately his shot hit the post, but it came back out to Alioski on the left. Alioski then smashed the ball into the net to give us that second goal.

I had no doubts that we would see the game out now, despite six minutes of injury time. I only realised their keeper had gone down after we had scored and he was receiving treatment. Shame on the Hull player for trying to get Bamford into bother afterwards by saying he had deliberately run into their keeper (you're too sh*t to play for Leeds comes to mind as I couldn't even remember him such was the lack of impact he made here). Replays later showed Bamford had swerved round the keeper without touching him. Get your facts right first I would say.

The win made this seven out of seven as Bielsa carries on emulating Don Revie. Thanks to Alison for buying one lucky person my new book *Marcelo Bielsa's Leeds United* as a Christmas present. Saturday sees another home game, this time against Cardiff. Well I aim to be there very early for this one as I am heading to the Merrion Centre first with my granddaughter Laura for the LUFC Trust AGM and also catching up with the new items in the centenary exhibition. See you there, LUFC – Marching on Together!

LEEDS UNITED V CARDIFF CITY 14 DECEMBER AT ELLAND ROAD

After missing kick-off last Tuesday, my granddaughter Laura and I were in Leeds just after 9am and parked up. We then headed up to the Merrion Centre for the LUFC Trust AGM and called in the Leeds shop there before it started, as I wanted one of the new dark blue training tops. Well done to the board of the trust for all the hard work they have done and are doing, especially as they are all volunteer Leeds fans. It was great seeing some of the new memorabilia on show and next weekend sees the last days for any Leeds fan to go and see it. After a quick trip to the German Christmas market for my bratwurst, we headed down for the special buses back to Elland Road as the heavens opened again.

On the way into the Peacock we found one of the helpers collecting for the children's heart surgery fund. As I had been given more money than the cost of my books on a couple of occasions recently that I had been asked to give to charity, I made sure that I put £10 into this fund as well as a couple of quid. Having had my daughter Charlotte die from congenital heart disease, this is definitely a worthwhile cause. Thank you to all the fans who bought my new book *Marcelo Bielsa's Leeds United* today, including some of our Norwegian fans. Anders, Terje, Edward, Vicky and Dave, your support is greatly appreciated. On the way into the ground we called into the East Stand entrance to drop off a couple of small bits for the toy appeal. With another bumper crowd for the last home game before Christmas, Leeds would have an unchanged team.

The team: Casilla, Ayling, White, Dallas, Berardi, Hernandez, Bamford, Harrison, Klich, Costa and Phillips. Subs: Nketiah for Bamford (77), Alioski for Harrison (81) and Struijk for Berardi (84). The game ended 3-3, with Costa (6) and Bamford (8 and a penalty 52) the Leeds scorers. Attendance was 34,552, with 710 Cardiff fans.

What a surprise it was to see Nikki leading the team out, with Rita the dog getting recognition for her fantastic support of Leeds United before her recent retirement. That was brilliant to see

and my daughter Danielle recognised her barking straight away. After Leeds had started on the attack, we had a great start to the game when we found ourselves two goals up within eight minutes. The first goal came after a breakaway attack when we cleared a Cardiff corner as Harrison came away with the ball. He passed out to Hernandez on the wing, who put a great pass across the field for Costa to run on to and put the ball into the net. The second one followed two minutes later after Dallas crossed the ball and Bamford scored to send the Leeds fans wild. Leeds had come close to getting a third goal before Cardiff had a chance. Leeds continued to press and won a free kick outside the area, but Bamford's shot went over the bar and later Ayling's shot was deflected and went past the wrong side of the post. Cardiff had three chances in the closing minutes of the half and Hernandez was denied a goal by their keeper. It had been a good first half and at times our one touch passing around the penalty area was fantastic to see as the team were cool, calm and collected.

At the start of the second half, Cardiff came out with more fight and looked more dangerous. Just as I was worried they could get into the game, Leeds had an attack. Bamford was brought down in the penalty area by their keeper and then scored from the penalty to give us some breathing space with a third goal. After nearly getting a fourth goal, Leeds let Cardiff back into the game when Casilla punched the ball out, only for their player to lob the ball back over him into the net. We'd had some passes going astray and then Bielsa made our first sub, with Bamford going off for Nketiah. Within five minutes Leeds were caught out as Cardiff scored a second goal. They had a

free kick, which caught everyone out as all our players congregated in the middle of the goal to defend it. Cardiff had a player on the touchline at the left-hand side of the pitch all on his own, so when the ball went straight out to him it wasn't expected to go there. He was in acres of space as he sent a cross into the penalty area for their player to head it into the net in the 82nd minute. As Cardiff threatened to get something out of the game, they had a player sent off in the 86th minute as he brought Nketiah down on the right wing with a bad foul. I hoped that would limit the threat from Cardiff, but unfortunately for us it didn't. As we had lost our height with Bamford going off, Bielsa made the decision to bring Struijk on which looked like he wanted to protect the lead and see the game out. It didn't work out the way we wanted it though, as I think it was a mistake to take Berardi off. Sadly, our defence seemed to be at sixes and sevens as two clashed for the same ball and within two minutes they got an equaliser to stun the Leeds support. With nearly the last kick of the game, Leeds were unlucky not to get a winner when their keeper made a fantastic save from Nketiah that hit White but went past the wrong side of the post.

That was a sucker punch today, having been so far in the lead then letting it slip. The aerial attacks and long throws had put us under pressure, and we didn't cope well with them. With having let in so little goals so far this season, we suddenly let in three in one game. The consensus as we came out of the ground was that Nketiah doesn't hold the ball up like Bamford does and we lose the ball very easily. It will have been a learning curve today because at times I thought we had become very complacent today. As usual we have to take the rough with the smooth, and despite feeling as if we had lost today, the positive is that we got a draw and one point. We are still in second place and in a good position with a 10-point gap behind us. There is a long way to go and there will be many unexpected scores for all clubs in the Championship still to come. We just need to keep on getting as many points as we can. Keep the faith and I'll see you at Fulham next week. LUFC – Marching on Together!

FULHAM V LEEDS UNITED 21 DECEMBER 2019 AT CRAVEN COTTAGE

First of all, I would like to wish all my readers a very Merry Christmas. Irrespective of the football result today, for those of you going through their own traumas, I wish you all the luck in the world and keep fighting. Having had a very challenging year for my family, I am looking forward to spending the time with them during my favourite time of the year.

Last Monday I was asked to take part in a Leeds United Centenary project that will take place in March. I have agreed to do this, and it was nice to hear that my name was put forward to join in by another couple of people. Thank you for recommending me, which is appreciated. Thank you to Kate, Sharon, Angela and Matt for buying my new book *Marcelo Bielsa's Leeds United*. For those of you who find this amongst your Christmas presents, enjoy the read and I look forward to receiving your feedback in due course.

With a 5am get up today for our trip to London, I picked Nikki and Annie her dog up to get the coach from Elland Road. I was chuffed to bits to see her lead the team out with Ayling last week, along with Rita who has now retired as a guide dog. It was good to see Rita get the send-off she deserved, having been an integral part of the Leeds support for so long. Tomorrow sees me take my three granddaughters to the Leeds United junior members Christmas party, so if you are going please ask for a photo.

We went straight to Putney Bridge on arrival in London and headed to Wetherspoons as usual. Imagine our surprise to be told we couldn't go in because we were Leeds fans! As we frequent the pub chain at every away game and have done for many a year, even getting told we are the best fans they have ever had in a couple of them, this was like a smack in the face. They said that the police had made this a home pub only. Their loss, especially as it was empty, and they were turning away our money. Merry Christmas? Bah humbug more like. We then walked over the Thames back to the other side and I said at least it wasn't raining and the sun was shining. I would regret saying that later when the heavens opened. Thank you to the Eight Bells who welcomed the Leeds fans with open arms – and their chicken and bacon roll tasted delicious. When Bryn, our Leeds policeman, arrived there to chat to fans, I mentioned we'd been turned away by the Rocket. He couldn't understand why they had made that a home pub and was going to have a word with them. It took us approximately ten mins to walk to the ground through the park where the rain had made massive puddles. We were asked eight times if we had got any spare tickets. Apparently, Fulham fans were selling tickets for £150 at the train station, which was an extortionate price.

We got in through the disabled entrance at the ground so was glad I didn't have to negotiate the narrow turnstiles that I came out of backwards last season. A nice lady steward helped me show Nikki to her seat at the front by the corner flag. Not really a good seat, which got wet and also had a sign on the pitch saying beware of flying balls. Not good when she is blind! I stayed with her until just before the kick-off, when her son Stephen arrived to sit with her. Because Fulham are rebuilding the stand to our left, which backs on to the Thames, this had reduced our allocation as we normally take up all the neutral seats too. It was disappointing to see the reaction of some of the Fulham stewards, which was a contrast to the lady we had met earlier. Some young lads had been pulled to one side, with the senior steward having a right go at them. I didn't see why he had pulled them to one side and thought he was trying to eject them at first, especially when he indicated they were mouthing off at him. This is where our stewards would have been good (Fulham refused to allow them to attend today) as they would have diffused the situation. A bit later, in the same area, I saw Ian, one of our members of the Griffin branch, trying to get down the steps to get out of the seating area to where the disabled area was. The next thing I saw was fans falling down the steps and a couple of punches being thrown. As someone was taken out, I assumed that's why it was kicking off, but could be wrong. The stand itself is dangerous as someone had already nearly fallen down the steps earlier when walking normally. Having a sign on some stewards saying 'Here to help' is obviously a misprint. All through the first half, fans from the lower part of the stand were sent out through the disabled entrance. When a Leeds fan who was recovering from a dislocated knee asked one steward at half-time if she could go out of the disabled entrance due to her injury, she was told no. She was told to get one of us Leeds fans to help her up the stairs instead. How callous and uncaring with a definite lack of Christmas spirit. My daughter Danielle helped her get up the stairs as she was on her own at the time. There was no need to make her do that at all, disgraceful.

Team: Casilla, Ayling, Harrison, Bamford, Hernandez, Phillips, Klich, Costa, Cooper, White and Dallas. Alioski for Hernandez (went off injured 3), Nketiah for Costa (45) and Stevens for Ayling (72). Leeds lost 2-1, with Bamford scoring for Leeds (54). Attendance was 18,878 with 1,900 Leeds fans. The referee today was a disgrace to the profession and should have been left in the dressing room at half-time. Inept, clueless, out of his depth, together with cheating, diving and time wasting from Fulham, meant we were up against it today.

Leeds started on the attack and their keeper made a save from a deflected shot. We had to then regroup when Hernandez pulled up injured in the third minute of the game, which meant he had to go off the pitch. Alioski came on to replace him but within four minutes we were a goal down when the referee awarded Fulham a soft penalty from which they duly scored. Both these incidents in a few minutes had given Leeds an uphill battle very early in the game. Despite this, I still thought we could get something from the game, but that was before the referee carried on with his ineptitude. When Fulham were falling down at the drop of a hat and time wasting that was bad enough, but their number nine led with his elbow three times and despite being spoken to wasn't booked, luckily for him, as he should have walked in the second half with a booking that should have been his second. There were plenty of angry fans around me who couldn't believe what they were witnessing; there again, it wasn't a surprise really. All I ask for is a level playing field and don't like to see cheating players falling down and conning the referee. To say they are supposed to be professionals, it's a shame they can't act that way. Fulham aren't the first team to play this way this season and no doubt won't be the last. Harrison was involved in two pieces of play where we came close to scoring. The first one saw their keeper save from Dallas, and Klich saw his shot come back off the post. Late in the half, Bamford saw their keeper make a save but the flag had also gone up for offside so it wouldn't have counted anyway.

The second half saw Nketiah had come in for Costa. I was looking forward to seeing how he played together with Bamford. When Fulham put the ball into our net at the opposite end of the ground, I'd seen the offside flag go up so was expecting it to be disallowed. Not long after this we got the breakthrough after Alioski put Nketiah through, and whilst his shot was parried it came to the feet of Bamford to smash the ball into the net to equalise. With both keepers in action after this, Alioski's header was saved before Fulham took a great shot that saw Casilla make a fantastic save. This was heading into the top left-hand corner looking at it from the away end, but I was confident that Casilla would be up to it. Unfortunately, Fulham did regain the lead shortly afterwards when the ball wasn't cleared, and they got the run of the ball to hit it into the net. Leeds did keep going until the final whistle blew and in the final minutes had another chance kicked off the line.

It wasn't to be, but there will always be ups and downs. I'll take the positives from the game that we are still in a good position in the table despite there being a long way to go. After a 17+ hour round trip, it was nice to get home after a very long day. Boxing Day sees the tea-time kick-off against Preston and another bumper crowd at Elland Road. We can do this Leeds, keep that positive mental attitude going into the next game. See you there, LUFC – Marching on Together!

LEEDS UNITED V PRESTON 26 DECEMBER 2019 AT ELLAND ROAD

I hope everyone has had a good Christmas. The start of the week saw the Junior Members' Christmas party at Elland Road. It turned out to be the most people I have seen attend this event over the last few years. Unfortunately, it meant there were queues galore for everything and, as they had to get more tables and chairs out, the disco and games were cancelled, which was a shame. The Christmas dinner was excellent though so well done for that.

I heard on Christmas Eve that my new book *Marcelo Bielsa's Leeds United* will be in the club shop in the New Year, which was great news. For those who received it for Christmas, including my sister Erica and nephew Steve, enjoy the read. A big thank you to Kate, Matt, Susan and Bremner for buying the book too as your support is greatly appreciated.

With it being a 5.15pm kick-off for Sky TV, I picked my granddaughter Hannah up early to allow plenty of time to get there. After a quick trip to the club shop and McDonalds we got into the Peacock with over three hours to spare, having met a young man from Greece who was attending his first game at Elland Road. We ended up sitting outside under the wooden seating area as I knew I wouldn't be able to stand up for that length of time. I'd started looking at my phone and realised someone had taken a photo of me for a change and turned around to find Chris laughing at me. That meant he had to have his photo taken too. Eventually Hannah and I were joined there by more of my family before heading into the ground. Once inside, as I stood talking to Susan, a young lad next to us and his friend started talking to us and immediately bought my book. By the time we had finished chatting it was nearly time for the game to start.

Team: Casilla, Ayling, Cooper, White, Alioski, Klich, Bamford, Harrison, Dallas, Costa and Phillips. Subs: Nketiah for Bamford (64). The game ended in a 1-1 draw, with Dallas equalising in the 89th minute. Attendance was 35,638, with 805 Preston fans.

With Preston playing in green and yellow, I kept thinking we were already playing West Bromwich Albion for some reason. For the first 20 minutes of the game, Preston put us under a lot of pressure, although we had started on the attack. Both Ayling and Cooper were guilty of putting passes across the pitch that were too short and were picked up by the Preston players, who were showing they wanted the ball more than us. There was a lot of sloppy passing going on as we struggled to get going. When Casilla went haring out of the area to get to the ball, he did have enough time to get to it. Unfortunately, he made a mess of the clearance and we were lucky not to get punished with a goal against us. I just thought Preston could have their ten minutes of play then we could take over the game, which didn't end up being the case. Preston weren't giving up as they constantly attacked us. We kept passing back to Casilla and no one was taking charge of the ball or looking like they wanted it at all. When we reverted to the long ball, especially from goal kicks, they were a waste of time as the ball never went to our players or was won by us. As Leeds attacked, we lost the ball, and with Preston players haring down on our goal I just knew they were going to score. After this they started with their time wasting and cheating antics of staying down with pretend injuries. At times we were bullied off the ball and Preston also showed their true colours early on when their answer to stopping us was to foul us. How some of their players didn't end up in the book early on was a mystery. I got a little worried that our players were going to get themselves in bother as they were very close to retaliating as well as some pushing and shoving. It was important that we didn't lose our cool, which is what Preston wanted. We did try getting back into the game with the last ten minutes of the half, but it had been a very poor 45 minutes for Leeds.

At the start of the second half, Cooper's first pass was too short again, which Preston took advantage of. You can always tell when things aren't going well on the pitch as there were plenty of expletives around us today. Things were starting to improve when Dallas brought a save out of the Preston keeper. The referee played on with two of the Preston players down on the floor, which I was glad about as it was about time they were ignored. Leeds had been attacking when Nketiah was standing at the side of the pitch ready to be brought on. As we were wondering who was going to go off as plenty of players hadn't been playing well, it flashed up on the scoreboard that Bamford was being replaced. Everyone around me was mystified as he had been getting involved in holding up play and making every effort to get involved and get the ball. There were plenty of boos around me when he went off, with one man saying that Bielsa had lost the plot. With our first attack after the substitution, Nketiah passed to Costa in the box and his cross went over Harrison and reached Alioski, whose shot sailed over the bar. That had been a good chance and when Nketiah's header was pushed around the post by the Preston keeper when it looked like a goal all the way, plenty began to think it wasn't going to happen for us today. With 15 minutes to go, it was very quiet around the ground for a couple of minutes as the realisation sank in, but then the Leeds fans got behind the team. The last minutes of the game belonged to Leeds as they went on the attack, looking for that equaliser. Alioski's shot hit the foot of the post and rebounded out, then Harrison's shot across the box put Preston under pressure and Alioski was denied once again, but this time by their keeper. On another day he could have had a hat-trick. Leeds were piling on the pressure when the ball came back out to Dallas on the edge of the area. He let fly with a deflected shot that went into the top of the net to send the Leeds fans wild as Elland Road erupted. Leeds were straight back to the middle of the park ready to get on with the game as they were looking for a winner. Although we kept on looking for the winner, in the end we had to settle for a draw. At least we didn't lose, and it didn't feel like a loss like the Cardiff game had as we got the late equaliser this time. Bielsa's decision to sub Bamford could be justified in the sense that we had some pace, attacked, and got a goal. Personally, I would have liked to have seen him stay on the pitch as well as Nketiah.

With a run of three away games to come with the visit to Birmingham and West Brom in the league and Arsenal in the FA Cup, none of these will be easy games. We will have to up our game, but I do feel the tactics at the start of the game today were not right. As well as our sloppiness, we let Preston dictate the game rather than us play to our strengths and let them worry about us. There was also too much playing back to Casilla today, which at times put us under pressure too. Onto our next game and for those of you who are going to Birmingham, I'll see you there, LUFC – Marching on Together!

BIRMINGHAM V LEEDS UNITED 29 DECEMBER 2019 AT THE ST ANDREW'S TRILLION TROPHY STADIUM

After spending three hours feeling sick and gipping during the night, I was glad when the feeling eventually subsided. Although this meant I had very little sleep, I decided to get up rather than have an extra half an hour in bed and take the dog for a walk before heading for Leeds. There was little traffic on the roads which was lovely, and I found myself parked up at the ground in plenty of time for the coach. I woke up just as we pulled up for our pub stop and was one of the first to get off the coach. As two of us queued up for a drink, I wondered where everyone else was. It turned out we had gone in the wrong pub, oh dear! When I eventually joined some of my friends, Keith said that if we won today then I would have to do the same when we play West Bromwich Albion on New Year's Day. It looks like I may have started something now after today's game, lol!

After the Birmingham fans caused trouble at the Elland Road fixture for our centenary game, it was Leeds fans who ended up punished for it with a reduced allocation of tickets and no beer on sale inside the ground today. Another club who use financial suicide when we could have sold the tickets three times over; it doesn't make sense to me. Thank you Phil 'Thumbsup' Cresswell for buying my new book *Marcelo Bielsa's Leeds United*.

Team: Casilla, Ayling, Cooper, White, Harrison, Klich, Nketiah, Phillips, Costa, Alioski and Dallas. Subs: Roberts for Nketiah (81) and Berardi for Klich (86). Leeds won the game 5-4, with goals from Costa (15), Harrison (21), Ayling (69), Dallas (84) and Harding own goal 90+5. Attendance was 22,059, with approximately 2,000 Leeds fans.

It was quite chilly as we waited at the tunnel at the right for the Leeds players to come out for their pre-game kickabout. As they went back inside, we headed to our seats in readiness for the start of the game. The teams then come out from the tunnel to the left of the stand, which I found weird.

I had no pre-conceptions about the game, just as always wanting us to win and get three points. I could never have imagined that within 21 minutes we would be leading 2-0. Our first goal came as we raced out of defence into attack and Harrison put Costa through, who slotted the ball home to put us into the lead. Six minutes later we went even further into the lead when Harrison's deflected shot ended up in the back of the net. At that point it looked like Birmingham were there for the taking. In true Leeds fashion, though, we weren't going to make things easy for ourselves. When three of our players went to mark one of theirs, it left an unmarked player on the left of the pitch to run towards our goal, pass it into the middle for them to pull a goal back. The game continued at a fast pace and before I knew it the whistle went for half-time with us leading 2-1.

It had been nice catching up with Gary Edwards, Collar and Rupert (one of my Selby Whites), so the game had already kicked off when I got back up into the stand. My heart sank when we didn't clear from a corner and Birmingham equalised. Two goals up and again we had thrown a lead away. If we thought that was the end of the goals, we were very much mistaken as this ended up being a game of goals galore. When Luke Ayling hit a fantastic shot from the edge of the box in front of us to put us 3-2 up to restore our lead, he was as over the moon as we were. Birmingham nearly scored an own goal from a Phillips corner but had their keeper to thank for keeping the ball out. He then saved from Alioski before the game turned once again as Birmingham equalised with a header. Damn, with Birmingham fans only waking up when they scored with their 'keep right on till the end of the road' song, then 'Leeds, Leeds are falling apart again', we shut them up within a minute. Leeds regained the lead when Ayling passed the ball for Dallas to bang it into the net. A day of our defence not clearing the ball and Casilla looking decidedly shaky showed when

Birmingham equalised for the fourth time in the first minute of injury time, making it 4-4, which looked to be the final score. More drama was to come though when we got a winner courtesy of an own goal, to send everyone in the away end wild. Berardi won the ball as Leeds powered forward and Ayling hit the ball hard across the area, which flew into the net from their player to give us a winner on the day. 5-4, who would have thought we would come out winners by that score? For once, though, we never let Birmingham take the lead as we always restored it as we had our shooting boots on today. Although we had been a little lightweight at times with our tackling, with Harrison and Costa getting pushed off the ball, the whole team showed a resilience and a never give up attitude which saw us get the win and three points to put us back to the top of the table. With this being our last game of the year, we stand proudly in a great position to go into the final countdown in our quest for promotion. I just want to wish everyone a Happy New Year and will see you at West Bromwich Albion on New Year's Day. Just on a poignant note, with 2019 a year that started badly for us as a family with my husband's cancer diagnosis, my daughter Danielle and I came out of the ground to the news that our chocolate Labrador Maisie had left us to go over the rainbow. She was the one who would not leave my husband alone, so he went to the doctors. I am glad 2019 is at an end now and look forward to a great 2020 where Leeds get promoted in our centenary year! LUFC – Marching on Together!

CHAPTER 7 – JANUARY 2020

WEST BROMWICH ALBION (WBA) V LEEDS UNITED 1 JANUARY 2020 AT THE HAWTHORNS

I hope everyone had a great start to the new year. Mine was 'chilling' in the hot tub with my granddaughters and looking forward to 2020. As WBA was a 5.15pm kick-off for Sky, we didn't leave Leeds until 11.00am on a lovely sunny day. As we headed down the M1, it didn't take long for the weather to become overcast and miserable. At our stop in Sutton Coldfield, it looks like we upset some of the locals. They weren't impressed with us as one said, 'Don't know why they're even in here when they're playing Albion, it's f**king miles away!' A pub stop with Leeds fans in it is why, lol!

As we got to the ground over an hour before kick-off, we went straight in. It was nice to have very friendly and chatty police officers treat us nicely, as well as their stewards. A big contrast to games in the 80s when fans used to be arrested for cheering when Leeds scored a goal. Give me days like today anytime. After chatting to many fans and taking their photos, I went to take one last one of Gary and the Shropshire Whites flag. In doing so, I nearly threw myself down the steps but regained my balance. Luckily, I'd put the strap for my camera around my wrist as it flew into the air, otherwise it would have become airborne.

Team: Casilla, Ayling, Alioski, Cooper, White, Klich, Dallas, Phillips, Nketiah, Costa and Harrison. Subs: Bamford for Nketiah (45) and Douglas for Alioski (45). The game ended in a 1-1 draw, with Bamford equalising for Leeds (52). Attendance was 25,618, with 1,989 Leeds fans.

The game was less than a couple of minutes old before WBA took the lead when the ball was deemed to have crossed the line when Leeds failed to clear it. They had won a corner; the ball was headed back across the goal and their player's attempt was awarded a goal despite Harrison clearing it off the line. Having heard this decision was inconclusive and another saying it had crossed the line, I'd like to see it again for myself. One thing, despite any differences with my opinion, it wouldn't change the goal being awarded. I found myself shaking when they scored and hoped it was because it was getting slightly colder. WBA came close again a short time later, but this time they hit the side netting. After we lost the ball in one incident, Bielsa looked to be getting frustrated on the side of the pitch. With Bamford on the bench, it was up to Nketiah to show what he could do, but for me he couldn't do the lone striker role. I kept screaming at him to go and put their keeper under pressure like Bamford does, but it took 30 minutes before he did that. We did get into the game more though, despite Casilla making some fantastic saves to prevent WBA going further into the lead. The nearest we had come to a goal was their keeper saving from Costa. There was no doubt in my mind, and those standing around me, that Nketiah was going to be replaced at half-time with Bamford, which proved to be the case. Douglas also came on to replace Alioski, which was another good decision.

We straight away looked stronger at the start of the second half with the substitutions and with Bamford putting players under pressure, we were getting the better of WBA. Harrison put a great ball over to the centre for Bamford to equalise within seven minutes of the restart with a deflected header. WBA came back at us straight away, but Casilla once again denied them a goal, before we counter-attacked with Bamford coming close to a second. Although WBA were always going to be a threat, Leeds continued to attack and we saw some brilliant moves, many with Harrison just in front of us and Costa at the other side. I felt we could get a winner at that time as we were getting on top and nearly did, but the flag went up for offside, although I'm sure that decision was wrong. Yes, I am biased, but seriously would like to see that one again. With Casilla making another save at the death, the game ended in a score draw, which was a good point today and meant we stayed at the top of the table.

Bartley came to clap the Leeds fans at the end of the game and Ayling was having a laugh with him. When WBA had been attacking our end in the first half, I'd seen Ayling winding him up. This game also turned out to be the last game Nketiah played for us as he has returned to Arsenal, cutting his loan spell short. He was a good super sub for me but his body language at times today showed his heart wasn't in it. I'd thought at the Birmingham game that he'd been the happiest I'd seen him for a while, probably because he'd made the decision to leave. With Clarke's loan also rescinded, with him returning to Spurs, we will find out soon enough whether we bring anyone else into the team.

With our FA Cup tie against Arsenal next, I for one still love the magic of the cup, regardless of those who chose to devalue the competition – either by writing us off, saying throw the towel

in, play the youngsters, rest the first team, it doesn't matter etc., well I disagree. The last few years have proved that being out of the cup gives no guarantees in getting promoted either, often proving detrimental to the cause. Winning breeds winning and having a good cup run could help us achieve our aim. I'll stand by that claim too, having seen how our best cup runs in the past have kept that fighting spirit going. As I am racing to the game after work, it will be touch and go to make it for kick-off, but I'm looking for everything to fall into place nicely with no stress. See you there, LUFC – Marching on Together!

ARSENAL V LEEDS UNITED 6 JANUARY 2020 AT THE EMIRATES – FA CUP THIRD ROUND

With an early morning appearance on BBC Radio Leeds talking about Leeds United and the FA Cup, I arrived a few minutes late for my slot. Then it was back to work before a very late set off for the game as the only way I could make it was to travel by train. I know everything about the day was going to be tight timewise, but arriving at the station ten minutes before the train was due to leave was too stressful for me. At least the train was on time, whereas a couple of the earlier trains were 30 minutes late due to cable issues in Leeds. I assumed this was something to do with the high winds that had appeared later that afternoon. It was a relief to be on the train and heading in the right direction. The next part that was to be a challenge for me was getting the underground to the game. Someone had pointed out to me earlier that I had been travelling to games in London for years, the only difference was that I have travelled by coach in recent times. It's a long time since we travelled by Wallace Arnold coaches in the 70s and had to make our own way to the grounds.

Just before the train arrived at Kings Cross, the conductor wished us good luck. A young lad started talking, saying he was jealous that we were going to the game and he had to watch it on TV. A woman and another man started talking to us about getting to the game too, which was nice. We had been given good instructions from Nikki about how to get to the ground due to the nearest stations being closed from 7pm, as we were arriving after that time. Her instructions were spot on, – thanks to her, as we were through the first set of barriers and on to the Victoria line in no time. As we were checking we were on the right platform, a Leeds fan came up to me to ask if I was the book lady and had I gone to Austria? As we chatted, I remembered the situation immediately as he had been on one of the buses to the ground when the German fans got on. The driver refused to let them travel and turfed them off, which was a good job as they'd clocked the lad and his mate as Leeds fans. It's a small world though, but as usual, where Leeds fans are concerned, we carried on chatting where we left off all those years ago. As we got off the underground with lots of other Leeds fans, luckily we had a good escort who knew where he was going. Even though everyone was heading in the same direction, it was good not to have to think where to find the ground. The one thing about the Emirates is that it looks impressive from the outside and is a big improvement on Highbury. Heading into the clock end was a far cry from the 70s where we used to be followed

by gangs of Arsenal fans around the stand trying to get away from them. One year everyone in front of me scattered and I was faced with some of their fans shouting, 'Come on,' trying to take Leeds fans on. That is one thing I don't miss for sure, as well as getting back to the coaches with no issues or getting ambushed in the café on Kings Cross station. There were massive queues getting into the ground as it was getting near kick-off, but there were plenty of singing Leeds fans about, with lots having been in London for hours before the game. There were some familiar faces around which was good to see, but plenty of new faces. For a great stand outside, the concourse inside and toilets I thought were extremely poor, especially trying to find out where the ladies were. I also prefer to be nearer the pitch no matter how impressive the ground looks from the stands. When I got to my seat someone was already in it, but as everyone was standing up it didn't really matter. It was nice to hear that Pontus Jansson, despite being sold, and Jack Clarke who had his loan period recalled, had come to support Leeds.

Team: Meslier, Ayling, Harrison, Klich, Phillips, Alioski, Douglas, Robbie Gotts (making his debut), Berardi, White and Bamford. Subs: Dallas for Gotts (60), Costa for Alioski (61) and Stevens for Ayling (78). Attendance was 58,403, with 8,000 Leeds fans. Leeds lost the game 1-0.

The first 45 minutes belonged to Leeds, and what a performance. We totally outclassed Arsenal as we took the game to them and were very unlucky not to have gone into an early lead. Both Meslier and their keeper were called into action before Bamford's great strike hit the crossbar. Leeds continued to get shots on target from both Harrison and White, which their keeper saved before Alioski's shot across the goal was agonisingly close. Arsenal had their keeper to thank for keeping them in the game, with further saves from both Harrison and Alioski. Gotts had a late chance but unfortunately the ball went over the crossbar, but he'd had a good debut. This had been a very impressive performance from Leeds United and the Leeds fans had also been outstanding in the library at the Emirates, putting their fans to shame. I'm sure I hadn't heard them singing until their first chant of 'Arsenal' in the 49th minute. Leeds had a sold-out allocation that could have been sold twice over as there were plenty of fans still looking for tickets before the game.

At half-time I was trying to find some fans from the Fullerton Park branch as we were travelling back on the coach with them, which was an easier option. At times I had struggled to see any familiar faces around me in the stand. As I am on the automatic ticket scheme, it meant I wasn't with the usual away season-ticket holders. Thank you Angie for pointing me in the right direction as it turned out they were just a few rows nearer the front than my seat. I felt happier knowing where the coaches were parked for after the game.

The second half saw Arsenal come out on the attack. As they had been humiliated in the first half, it looked like they'd had a rollicking from their new manager. The referee had let a lot of things go during the game, some which had been to our advantage, which I thought were justified, but this included some tackles on our players that should have been punished. They then started falling over very easily, winning a free kick just outside the area which then hit the crossbar.

Meslier had been having a great game and I was very impressed with him. I felt completely at ease with his distribution and the saves he made. Unfortunately, when they scored, they got the luck of the green when the ball deflected to their player just in front of Meslier to put the ball into the net. Just before that, Bamford had another shot saved by their keeper. Leeds tried to get back into the game and never gave up, but on the day they couldn't get the ball into the net. Sadly for me, Costa was very poor when he came on as sub. I'm not sure if he was playing out of position but he looked very lightweight with no conviction. The positives were that we had plenty of shots on target that brought saves out of their keeper and played some great Bielsa ball. I'm very proud to be a Leeds fan as always and we put up a great show to the world with our great performance.

As I was waiting downstairs after the game, it was nice to see lots of familiar faces there amidst the singing Leeds fans. Suddenly to the right of me, I heard a commotion as things started to kick off. It looked like one of the police had hit a Leeds fan which started it off. I heard afterwards that a lad had been banging on the kiosk with the 'pump it up' song when he was man handled and thrown to the floor. Maybe he shouldn't have been banging on it, but I don't think there was any need to react the way the police did, which was way over the top. I think the lad was still on the floor as I left the ground but not sure if he'd been arrested.

Back to the league with the game against Sheffield Wednesday on Saturday, but we can use the momentum and the high feeling of putting in a great performance to go on a good run. Keep fighting Leeds with the best fans in the world and I'll see you there. LUFC – Marching on Together!

LEEDS UNITED V SHEFFIELD WEDNESDAY 11 JANUARY 2020 AT ELLAND ROAD

It took a while to get going this morning but as I knew that I'd got an excited little girl waiting to be picked up, I had to get a move on. Alexis couldn't wait to wear her new Leeds United kit she got for Christmas. She said she was never going to take it off and, as she looked so cute in it, I knew what she meant. There were plenty of queues of traffic along Elland Road two hours before kick-off, which quite surprised me. A new park and ride from Junction 45 of the M1 was being trialled today, which, although the opposite direction from us, should be a good thing to ease congestion around the ground in the future. After a visit to the Peacock first we headed into the ground in good time. As we stood outside the Kop entrances getting our bags searched, a police bike skidded past on the other side of the fence. A few seconds later a double decker bus appeared with everyone banging on the windows and going mad. It's a good job the windows stayed intact otherwise lots of the Wednesday fans would have met the tarmac with a bang! For once they had sold all their tickets for the game.

Team: Casilla, Cooper, White, Dallas, Douglas, Bamford, Costa, Klich, Phillips, Harrison and Ayling. Subs: Alioski for Douglas (56), Hernandez for Klich (66) and Stevens for Costa (75). Attendance was 36,422 with 2,644 Wednesday fans. Leeds lost the game 2-0.

I didn't read a lot of the comments on social media as it looked like many had already made their minds up about today's game, and not in a good way. It was better to go with a clear mind and as usual make my mind up about what I see on the pitch. With Garry Monk back once again with the opposition I thought we wouldn't let him get the better of us again. Sadly, I was wrong. The first thing that went against us was being turned around to attack the Kop in the first half. Now I assumed that we had lost the toss but have read on social media since that we won the toss, meaning Cooper turned us around? Hopefully, someone will clarify if that was the case. I'm sorry, I don't care if it was to take advantage of the wind, and if that was the reason then it gave us a psychological disadvantage as we should always kick towards the Kop in the second half from our perspective.

Leeds started brightly enough with a couple of off-target shots, before Wednesday had a chance with a header that was off target too, before another chance was put wide. Bamford brought a save out of their keeper before Harrison had a great chance that went past the post. There was some lovely footwork, where we ran rings round some of the Wednesday players, and when Harrison passed the ball through to Klich the linesman put his flag up as Bamford's header hit the back of the net. Apparently, it was Klich who was offside in the build-up. Once again Bamford had the ball in the net, only to see a goal disallowed. Their keeper kept Wednesday in the game just before half-time with saves from Harrison and Bamford. Costa's late chance was blasted over the bar as we went in on equal terms. The atmosphere on the terraces had been quiet at times and I just wanted us to sing and get behind the team. It felt like there was a lot of anxiousness on the terraces, which I didn't want to affect the players.

The second half saw Bamford with a great chance after Costa crossed from the byline but this time the chance didn't go his way. Wednesday had a similar chance shortly after, before nearly taking the lead from a corner. Even though we had a player on the line marking one of theirs, Casilla scooped the ball out from over their heads. Leeds still had chances, which didn't come to fruition, and their keeper saved from Klich. The atmosphere was a lot better in the second half. When Alioski was ready to come on as sub, I thought it was going to be Douglas going off. He seemed to be very slow with some of his judgements today, although he didn't play badly. Cooper started doing that a bit later too, even though we were still managing to create spaces. When Wednesday started dropping like flies, it was good to see the referee refusing to let their trainers onto the field. A couple of good decisions there to stop time wasting by the opposition. Just after that, Bannan's cramp miraculously disappeared as he ran to the opposite end of the field, so it was a good decision for once. Their first goal came after White had won the ball and was running forward with it before losing it. Cooper ran back to mark their player and I thought if he'd just stayed where he was their player may have been offside. Unfortunately, he ran on and beat Casilla at the near post to put them into the lead three minutes from time. With five minutes of stoppage time and the Leeds fans roaring the team on, I was hopeful of an equaliser. When Wednesday got the ball on the right-hand side and crossed it, the lad beside me said 'this is the second,' which it turned out to be. Well and truly beaten in the end, which is football sadly. I didn't think they were better than us on the day, but we need to put our chances away. If Bamford's goal had stood in the first half it could have been a different game but wasn't to be. Lots of Leeds fans have got a déjà vu feeling about the season, but that depends on whether anyone is brought in during the transfer window. I'm not accepting defeat at this stage of the season as there is still a long way to go, but there were plenty of boos around us at the end of the game as we stayed until the bitter end. All we can do at this moment in time is wait and see what happens and be there to support them as we do.

Having met some Irish fans who had left home at 5am this morning for the game, we will be in the same position next week for our visit to QPR. With it being a 12.30pm kick off, it means another long day for us travelling to London. With another sell-out crowd from the Leeds fans, our loyalty is second to none. See you there, LUFC – Marching on Together!

QPR V LEEDS UNITED 18 JANUARY 2020 AT THE KIYAN PRINCE FOUNDATION STADIUM

After getting home from my brother's birthday party in the early hours, I found that despite trying to get a few hours' sleep before heading to QPR, I found I was wide awake. To ensure I didn't oversleep, I got up at 3am and headed to Elland Road for the coach. Luckily, I managed to sleep most of the way there and back. We managed to have a pub stop in Uxbridge before arriving at the ground in time for kick-off. With the upper away end having to be accessed at the far side of the ground, we had a nice walk in the sunshine, despite a frosty morning. My flag, hung up at the back of the stand, made its first return to a game after being at the recent LUFC Trust Exhibition.

Team: Casilla, Ayling, Cooper, White, Klich, Harrison, Costa, Bamford, Phillips, Hernandez and Dallas. Subs: Alioski for Dallas (45) and Stevens for Klich (87). Leeds lost the game 1-0 with Phillips getting sent off with a straight red card. Attendance was 16,049, with 2,973 Leeds fans. Jack Clarke made his loan debut from the subs bench for QPR after ending his recent loan spell from Spurs at Leeds.

QPR had some big players who bullied us off the ball, getting their first shot of the game in the opening minutes, which Casilla saved. Within three minutes, Leeds should have had a penalty when Costa was brought down in the area with a strong challenge, but the referee waved play on. Bamford had a long-range shot trying to beat their keeper, who was out of his area, but the shot went wide. Leeds were unlucky not to take the lead when a free kick brought a save out of their keeper, which had deflected off one of their players. There had been quite a few strong challenges from QPR on our players, which should have brought an early booking for at least a couple of them. Leeds went behind in controversial circumstances when QPR won a free kick on the edge of our penalty area. As Casilla lined the wall up, I couldn't believe he was standing at the left-hand side of the goal with a massive space to the right of him that wasn't covered by anyone. There should have been at least one of our players on the right-hand post for me. As it was, when their player got the ball, it hit both his hands before he put the ball into the net. Even though we appealed, the goal was allowed to stand with boos from the Leeds fans ringing out. The linesman should have picked that up, and also when Dallas nearly had his shirt ripped off his back, but he was half asleep and missed them both. I still don't understand how Dallas came to be booked for the latter incident. It took until the 35th minute for one of their players to be booked for a foul, when plenty of heavy challenges had already taken place. When we had a corner, the balls were always picked up in the middle by the QPR players as I shouted for us to hit it hard and low instead to catch them out. Bamford had a shot saved by their keeper and a second chance went over the crossbar as we went into the break a goal behind.

Alioski replaced Dallas at the start of the second half as Leeds started on the attack. Although we had some good possession, we couldn't get that breakthrough until Bamford was brought down in the penalty area by their keeper. With the penalty being taken by Bamford, I was hesitant when he took a long run up to the ball. Unfortunately, the low shot to his right was saved by their keeper. Damn, that was the best chance we had to score. As Leeds tried to get something out of the game, shots went wide, but Hernandez came close with a free kick. It just felt like we weren't going to get a goal, despite having lots of possession. Lots of fans were getting frustrated and blaming Bamford for not scoring, saying he should have done better with his chances. As far as I'm concerned, he cannot do it on his own. When Roberts came back into the side, that was when things worked for Bamford. He needs an Allan Clarke alongside him to put the ball into the net. In the closing minutes Phillips got his marching orders with a straight red card in the 88th minute after a bad tackle saw the frustrations creep into his play. He will now be banned for three games. The game ended with our ten men not being able to get an equaliser.

With fans clamouring for reinforcements since Nketiah and Clarke left to go back to Arsenal and Spurs respectively, the pressure is on the club not to have a repeat of last season's capitulation. Radrizzani had been in the director's box in the first half but didn't appear for the second half, and later in the game Orta was slumped in his seat when we couldn't get that equaliser. Personally, I had that resigned feeling today, but all is not lost as we are still in a good position, with others around us losing points too. We have a break next Saturday due to the Millwall game being rearranged for the following Tuesday due to their involvement in the FA Cup. Keep the faith no matter how hard it is, see you there, LUFC – Marching on Together!

LEEDS UNITED V MILLWALL 28 JANUARY 2020 AT ELLAND ROAD

Apologies for the delay for those of you who are waiting to read my blog. Despite having a weekend free with this re-arranged game due to Millwall being involved in the fourth round of the FA Cup, Leeds United's social media channels have seen our fans going into overdrive. If it wasn't TOMA (take over my arse), it was transfers, or lack of them according to some. With the talk of investment coming into the club from QSI, this coincided with incoming transfers of Elia Caprile, a goalkeeper from Italian club Chievo Verona, and 19-year-old Ian Poveda, a winger from Manchester City, both

on permanent deals. The message boards went into overdrive with the incoming of Jean-Kevin Augustin, whose loan deal with Monaco from RB Leipzig was cut short so he could be loaned to Leeds for the rest of the season. I thought we would have a feel-good factor around Elland Road due to these signings and was looking forward to the game.

As I'd been at a meeting in Castleford all day, my daughter Dani was picking up my granddaughter Hannah, so I got to the ground for 6pm. I decided to go into the club shop for a new lanyard, which turned out to be a very expensive trip courtesy of early Easter presents for two of my granddaughters, Hannah and Alexis. Whilst in the shop I was pleased to see that my new book *Marcelo Bielsa's Leeds United* had arrived in stock and signed those on display for them. I went to the Peacock and was introduced to George, who had gone to extraordinary lengths to get to Elland Road for the recent Boro game. He was coaching in America and had to take a four-hour train journey to New York then walk to Penn station. From there he travelled by train to Newark airport to get a plane to Iceland and another one to Manchester. When he arrived there, he found out his train to Leeds was cancelled, so he got the bus to Elland Road where he eventually met up with his dad in the Peacock. It was all worth it though when Leeds won the game 4-0, but it just shows what Leeds fans do to support their team. I then met my niece Sonya and headed into the ground in time for kick-off.

Team: Casilla, Ayling, Cooper, White, Hernandez, Bamford, Dallas, Costa, Alioski, Harrison, and Klich. Sub: Shackleton for Hernandez (90+4). Leeds won the game 3-2 with goals from Bamford (48 and 66) and Hernandez (62) after going two goals down. Attendance was 34,006, with 471 Millwall fans.

Millwall started on the attack and put us under pressure in the opening moments of the game. They won an early corner and the referee decided to have words with Alioski and a Millwall player. As Alioski chased their player around Casilla, the ball was sent over their heads to another one at the far post with no one marking him, who headed the ball into the net in the fourth minute. Damn that was just what we didn't need, and bottles rained down on Millwall as they celebrated in front of the Leeds fans. As Leeds started to attack, we had a couple of players brought down, which despite looking like bad tackles were waved play on by the referee. Lo and behold when one of the Millwall players was brought down with a tame tackle, the referee immediately blew for a free kick to Millwall. With both Alioski and Klich going close and Bamford having a shot saved by their keeper as we tried to get an equaliser, the referee surpassed himself well and truly. With Leeds fans in the South Stand shouting for a corner, I couldn't comment as I didn't see the resulting shot. When the replay was shown on the scoreboard, the whole ground was in uproar as Dallas's great shot was saved by their keeper, but instead of a corner the referee gave a goal kick! That was when I realised once again that we were playing the officials and their absolute biased approach is a disgrace to the profession. Even the linesmen got in on the act by not flagging for the ball going out, and as Millwall played on they won a penalty. When I saw Klich walking over to the bench I thought he'd been sent off at first, but he'd gone for a drink. I was convinced it wasn't a penalty as their player fell over in the area and have heard conflicting reports both for and against it being awarded in the first place. Cooper had a header saved by their keeper and as half-time approached the terraces quietened down. There was a round of applause on the 36th minute for Leeds fan Danny Rahnavard who had recently died suddenly, and his son Olly was going to be in his dad's seat for the game. This was to celebrate his life but also to show his son that Leeds United are a family. I said we needed a goal on either side of half-time to get back into the game but went into the break 2-0 down. I didn't think they were two goals better than us though, despite the score.

There was plenty of talk about the dismal performance of the referee, especially as the officials don't hide their dereliction of duty anymore. Having seen Leeds suffer with bad decisions by the officials more times than I care to remember over the years, it really feels like they have an agenda to keep us down in this league as we are the cash cow for the division. A couple of lads I know said they had a 3-2 bet on for Leeds to win and I said I'd go for that.

Leeds had come out early for the second half and immediately were on the attack as the whistle blew. I didn't get the prediction of a late goal in the first half right, but the one straight after half-time happened. With a corner sent over to the middle by Hernandez, their keeper saved from Harrison, but Bamford was on hand to put the rebound into the net to pull a goal back. Leeds continued to attack with intense pressure and played some lovely football. Costa, who had been quiet in the first half, put on a good show with some great attacking and Klich was also very impressive as Leeds fought to get an equaliser. Their keeper was forced into action to save from Bamford, Hernandez and Harrison to keep us out. Alioski came close to an equaliser before Millwall had another attack. Leeds were on fire with waves of attacking, and when Hernandez's shot hit the back of the net to equalise Elland Road erupted. Game on now as we went for the winner, which came four minutes later when Bamford got his second goal of the game by heading the ball into the net to send everyone wild! Elland Road was bouncing, and the noise was out of this world as well as the euphoria of coming back from two goals down to lead. Casilla had to be on the alert to keep Millwall out, but I was adamant they were not going to score. When they won a corner, Millwall took ages before they took it, but not before one of their players complained to the referee and handed something to him. I took it that someone had thrown something at him whilst waiting to take the corner. We can't give the EFL any further ammunition to have a go at us, so please think before you throw things on the pitch. Leeds had a great chance to put the game to bed when Klich received the ball on the edge of the box in acres of space but sank to his knees as he blasted the ball over. That was such a shame as he deserved a goal today. As the whistle blew to end the game, the Leeds fans cheered and gave the team a standing ovation as they went around and off the pitch. We also returned to the top of the league with other results going our way and with this important win!

After the game we met my sister Erica and her boyfriend Martin at Billy's statue, and at least he got his birthday present of a win. Although my hands were cold, my heart was on fire with love for Leeds United before we headed home very happy. See you on Saturday for the Wigan game, LUFC – Marching on Together!

CHAPTER 8 – FEBRUARY 2020

LEEDS UNITED V WIGAN 1 FEBRUARY 2020 AT ELLAND ROAD

With high winds and an icy chill factor, we headed to Elland Road for the game. Due to some fans making mischief on WACCOE with the kick-off time, I decided I'd better check for myself just to make sure it was 3pm. Whilst my granddaughter Laura was having something to eat in McDonalds, I felt really tired and could have gone to sleep. As we came out of there, a man coming towards me said, 'It's Heidi isn't it?' To which I responded that it was. He remembered me going onto the Gelderd End in 1974. When I realised that was 46 years ago, I wondered where the time had gone, especially when I've said I'm 35 for so many years.

In the Peacock I was chatting with the Goole Whites and reminiscing about travelling with the Selby Whites when I ran the supporter's club branch. Our coach in those days started off in Goole, then to Snaith, Carlton, Selby, Monk Fryston and Sherburn before we set off to the away games, also picking up some of our RAF lads at Doncaster. We had a very loyal set of fans who went everywhere, and it's always nice to catch up with them. Thank you to Mick Glasby, one of our Nottingham Whites, for buying my book *Marcelo Bielsa's Leeds United*, and I appreciate the support. From there we went to the club shop, and whilst in there I got chatting to a man who said I used to travel with them on the Hull coach when Rowan ran it. A few others started talking about me being in the Leeds United documentary *Take us Home* as well as my books and thank you for all your comments, which are appreciated. A lad was handing out leaflets for a comedy-drama at the City Varieties called Billy Bremner & Me by Phil Differ. This will take place on Friday, 17 April, tickets are £18. Follow @events105 on Facebook for further details. I am looking forward to going to this as Billy Bremner always was and always will be my hero. After going to the front of the Kop to get my customary photos and chatting to other Leeds fans, we got to our seats as the game kicked off.

Team: Casilla, Ayling, Cooper, White, Dallas, Klich, Harrison, Costa, Bamford, Hernandez and Alioski. Sub: Roberts for Alioski (64). Leeds lost the game 1-0. Attendance was 35,162, with 519 Wigan fans.

The winds were still swirling, which was going to impact on the game today, but I had high hopes for us to do well. Leeds started off brightly enough and, with a bit of luck, would get something out of the game. Harrison beat their keeper with a shot but was very unlucky when it hit the post and bounced back out again. Wigan looked strong and were always a threat. When they won an early corner, I was watching who Alioski was marking on the line and looking out for stragglers on their own, but we didn't have a replica of Millwall's first goal thank goodness. For some reason I didn't feel comfortable watching through my glasses today, whether it was because it was so dull, I'm not sure. It was even worse taking them off as I couldn't make players out so used

FOLLOW ME AND LEEDS UNITED

LEEDS

LEEDS UNITED

100 YEARS

LEEDS	
13	K. CASILLA
2	L. AYLING
5	B. WHITE
6	L. COOPER
9	P. BAMFORD
15	S. DALLAS
17	H. COSTA
19	P. HERNANDEZ
22	J. HARRISON
23	K. PHILLIPS
43	M. KLICH

STARTING XI

my camera to zoom in instead. We got into some good positions but were unable to convert any chances. Bamford had moved out wide and put a great cross in, but Harrison was unable to put the ball into the net and Costa put another chance just over the top. Some other chances were way off target though, with an Alioski shot hitting the top of the stand. With some fans getting frustrated that we hadn't hit the target, I thought the wind was playing havoc with some of the play. Wigan won a free kick at the edge of the box and the resulting shot hit the side netting as we went into the break level. It hadn't been the best of halves, despite having lots of possession.

Downstairs, at half-time, my friend Margaret said that four Spanish fans from Madrid had come into the Peacock after I'd left looking for tickets for the game. They said as there were Leeds fans everywhere there were no tickets to be found. They had followed Leeds for a long time but were also Bielsa fans (one was wearing an Argentina shirt under his jumper). Margaret told them their best bet was to go around the ground and see if there were any to be found. I said that I would have headed to the main entrance, told them they were Bielsa fans from abroad and see if they could get in. In fact, they could have sneaked them in with the Wigan fans as there were plenty of spare seats there!

The second half saw us start off on the attack again, with some fans castigating Bamford when his header was off target. At least he was getting in the position to have a chance in the first place. Wigan headed a chance off the line for us and then they had an attack and won a corner. I zoomed in to see what was happening as the ball went across to the middle. The next thing the ball was nestling in the back of the net as I wondered why Casilla hadn't had command of his area. Apparently, the ball took a deflection, but I'd like to see the incident again to see what exactly happened. Time-wasting tactics started appearing, with Wigan players going down like a sack of spuds time after time. I'd be much happier to see these players taken off the pitch and let the game carry on because half of the time there is nothing wrong with them, which infuriates me. In comparison, any fouls on our players saw them get up without any trainers coming on to the pitch. Leeds fans shouted for a penalty with a handball, but we were awarded a corner instead. Unfortunately, with heads from fans in front of me, I didn't see it as it was at the far side of the goal and my view was blocked. It was nice to see Roberts come on as sub as we started attacking down the flanks but had no luck when the ball came into the centre of the box. Wigan brought a sub on to calm things down, which was their prerogative, but it took the sting out of the game. We had to keep going and not give up, and even though I was desperate for us to score, deep down I think I knew it wasn't going to happen. The longer the game went on, the more it felt like the ghost of last season's defeat, which was the catalyst for us not getting automatic promotion, was having an impact. Wigan were waiting to break when our attacks broke down, and with one they were through and it looked like they had only Casilla to beat when Leeds won the ball back. They had come close before that when they had the rub of the green, but Leeds fought to get the ball back off them to start another attack. We didn't give up despite lots of the passing across the goal not coming off, and were very unlucky in the last minute of the game when Bamford's header was cleared off the line and Costa's shot then went over. It wasn't to be, but loads of fans booed at the end of the game, which I find very sad. I know it's a kick in the teeth when we are beaten and it hurts, but I still believe in Bielsa and the team.

There are always going to be ups and downs and we are still in there. After the euphoria at the end of the game on Tuesday, it was back down to earth with a bang today, but fingers crossed the blips will be outdone by us continuing to play good football.

Laura was very excited when I asked her if we should go round to the players' entrance after the game, despite the icy wind. As we stood there, I got talking to some fans who followed me on Facebook about the documentary and then got talking to some others. There were a lot of fans waiting as this man came to the fence and shouted for everyone to get out of the way to let a van in. Someone shouted to him, 'Where is the please, when there are loads of kids here waiting?' I was astounded with the man's reply, saying that he didn't need to, which had everyone shaking their heads. He was so arrogant it was unbelievable. As the man behind me said, 'You stupid, stupid man not saying please when there are kids about,' it obviously hit a chord because the next time he shouted something out he said please. There is no need at all to treat any of our fans with disdain, especially as we are all paying customers. With other club employees around there being so nice, maybe he's got too big for his boots? I managed to get photos of Laura with a few of the players before we left as she was cold so we had to head home. I had to laugh as she'd told me not to take too many photos of her today, but she was very happy to pose with the players, especially Jamie Shackleton, her favourite player!

Next Saturday sees us head to Nottingham for the tea-time kick-off at Forest. We can and we will keep fighting. See you there, LUFC – Marching on Together!

NOTTINGHAM FOREST V LEEDS UNITED 8 FEBRUARY 2020 AT THE CITY GROUND

Last week's defeat by Wigan saw social media once again go into meltdown. Fans are entitled to their opinions and I learnt a long time ago that there will always be lots of differences in them. What I do find very sad though is how toxic it became when I started to read a lot of the comments. Bielsa will not get everything right that's for sure, but those calling for his head is something I cannot agree with. There is still a long way to go and I still have hope and belief that we can turn this around. With the result going against us again today, the social media side will not be any better this week.

After stopping in Mansfield, we got to the ground 30 minutes before kick-off, getting dropped off outside the turnstiles. One thing that surprised me was getting straight into the ground without the pre-requisite bag searches, which for once were missing. My flag was hung up near the front of the stand, which I could see from my seat, which was next to the divide between the two sets of fans.

Team: Casilla, Ayling, Cooper, Dallas, Klich, Alioski, White, Hernandez, Bamford, Costa and Harrison. Subs: Roberts for Hernandez (59), Shackleton for Alioski (70) and Jean-Kevin Augustin making his debut for Bamford (71). Leeds lost the game 2-0. Attendance was 29,455, with 1,993 Leeds fans.

As the game kicked off, this was the noisiest I have ever heard them at the City ground. The flag waving and record playing got their fans wound up, plus of course they were playing Leeds United! With Forest starting on the attack, Casilla was called into action twice to make the saves. They looked a strong side, winning some corners, which saw man marking around Casilla, leaving him with no room. Leeds had an attack which ended with Alioski's shot deflecting wide, although I didn't realise that as I was surprised to see we'd got a corner from it. Not long after that, Forest took the lead. Hernandez's pass was poor, and Forest took advantage by winning possession and running towards us. When their player was in the penalty area looking to cross the ball, instead he took a shot that went past Casilla's near post and into the net. He really shouldn't have been beaten with that shot, although it was very powerful. That was the score as we went into the break.

The second half saw us start with no changes as Leeds attacked towards the goal in front of the Leeds fans. A counter-attack by Forest saw them nearly double their lead but although in loads of space, their final shot was saved by Casilla. Roberts came on as sub and I hoped that playing alongside Bamford would help. Unfortunately, the first tackle on Roberts saw him injured and reports from some fans after the game indicated that he left on crutches, which isn't a good sign. Augustin came on in place of Bamford, which was a shame as I'd like to see us try two strikers up front. Alioski had to go off for me as the Forest players were gunning for him and I thought he would get sent off otherwise. It was nice to see Shackleton come on as sub too. Augustin won a

183

corner and you could almost feel the panic in the Forest defence as they didn't know what to do with him. Cooper's header was very close to going over the line as Forest cleared it. Leeds were trying to get something out of the game as they attacked the goal in front of us. A ball boy to the right of us walked very slowly with the ball and then put it on the floor to waste time rather than give it to our player for a throw in. We kept getting caught offside, but one was really annoying as a Forest player handled the ball on the wing first and we didn't get the free kick we should have had. There was always a danger we could concede a second goal, but I was hoping to get at least a draw out of the game. As it was, with another counter-attack, Harrison was bundled off the ball by two of the Forest players as they ran to the far end and scored a second goal at the death. Harrison had been the last man but wasn't strong enough to take on two players. That sent the Forest fans next to us wild as they surged towards the Leeds fans. Just before the end of the game, one of the Forest stewards indicated to me not to take any photos as our stewards wondered what was going on. I decided to go and get my flag and as I got to the front of the stand the final whistle blew. A few minutes after the end of the game, I was standing with my back to the Forest fans as a coin hit my head. Idiots, and apparently they'd been doing that all game. My beret came in handy as it saved me from an injury but a lad earlier had got a right bruise from one hitting him. All our disabled fans were in that area too which makes it even worse for me. To hear that they had to go through the baying Forest fans to get out of the ground wasn't good either. Luckily, their fans were cleared to make way for them.

Back on the coach there was a lot of resignation from the Leeds fans, especially with the trip to Brentford next. After being shown Ayling's interview after the game, I thought he looked close to tears and was very down. Bielsa had listened to the fans and I thought the subs made us look stronger, but we were beaten in the end by two breakaway goals. Just don't give up Leeds, but maybe we need a bit of reverse psychology. We are not challenging for automatic promotion so forget it and take the pressure off yourselves. LUFC – Marching on Together!

BRENTFORD V LEEDS UNITED 11 FEBRUARY 2020 AT GRIFFIN PARK

Leeds fans are at their best when we are all on the same page with that siege mentality. Now, more than ever, we need to get that back despite results or differences of opinions. Keep fighting, never say die and do our best to get that spine-tingling atmosphere back, which I love. The team will know we are behind them and must also never give up. We must still believe, and I am not ready to throw the towel in yet.

The one thing that has really upset me this last week is seeing that our older fans are getting the blame for the dire atmospheres and being told to stop going to away games. Eventually I got so riled up I had to say something. Those who have built up their loyalty over years and years, through thick and thin, through good and bad times, should roll over and let others have their tickets? Not in a million years should that happen and I for one am not going to relinquish my ticket.

Whether the demographic change of our support has something to do with things changing I am not sure, but loyal fans getting the blame is not the way to do it. Our support has stood up over the years, which is why we have the worldwide fan base that we have, and their loyalty should be acknowledged. Embrace what we have because we do know for certain that if things do change for the worse again, those fans will still be there regardless. We are going to do this, come on Leeds. Someone passed me in the seats and said he'd stuck up for me so I'm assuming it was to do with this.

Team: Casilla, Ayling, Cooper, Klich, Dallas, Phillips, Costa, White, Harrison, Hernandez and Bamford. Sub: Augustin for Bamford (76). Leeds drew 1-1 with Cooper getting our goal (39). Attendance: 12,294 with 1,400 Leeds fans.

My message to Leeds before the game was that I was still behind Bielsa, Leeds should keep fighting and never say die. The team should prove the doubters wrong, starting with Brentford. I'm glad my pep talk worked lol! Seriously though, I'm still going to believe we can do this however hard it is. Leeds tonight produced a great fighting performance and the psychological boost of gaining a point and coming away from the game playing well will be immense.

On arrival at the ground just before kick-off, I immediately recognised someone from the past, a Goole White. I'm not sure how long ago it was that we travelled to away games, but I never forget a face. That came in useful in the 70s and 80s when things were very hairy for us fans on the terraces, especially if you were surrounded by the opposition fans. Seeing a familiar face was good, even if you had to pretend you were not a Leeds fan, so they did not get sussed. Ask me what happened yesterday, and I don't stand a chance of remembering lol. The lad next to me had messaged his mate saying that he was sat next to me. When his mate said watch out for the camera, he was too late as I'd already taken his photo, oops!

Although the first chance of the game fell to Brentford, Leeds started well, having plenty of possession, and when Harrison cut in from the wing beating a few Brentford players he got into a good position to shoot, only for his final shot to lack power. Phillips was back after his recent suspension and he is pivotal in the way we play, and his performance tonight was immense. Leeds continued to dominate but another chance lacked power and their keeper saved it very easily. When Brentford did get a chance to shoot, it looked as if it was on target and going in, but luckily for us it whizzed past the outside of the post. Leeds started passing across the back after previously using our best form of defence – attack. This came back to haunt us shortly afterwards as Cooper passed the ball back to Casilla, only for him to slip and let their player in to score. After having a fantastic atmosphere on the terraces, that was like a kick in the teeth having dominated the game so far. The Leeds fans picked themselves up again, getting behind the team, as Brentford looked for a second goal, but Ayling defended well and blocked for a corner. As Leeds stepped up their attack again, we won a corner at the far end of the pitch. As we don't usually do well from corners, it was great when Cooper got on the end of Harrison's corner to put the ball into the net. Leeds ran back

to the centre to get straight on with the game as the Leeds fans celebrated. Leeds ended up on the attack as the whistle blew for half-time, but they had played well and deserved to be on level terms at the break, having gone a goal down. Leeds were also the better team.

The second half started quietly before Leeds broke away on a counter-attack, with Costa and Klich playing a great one-two between them, but their keeper saved Costa's shot. Leeds started to ramp up the pressure down the flanks, with both Harrison and Costa starting to battle and beat their man as Leeds started to look for a winner. Brentford were finding it hard to get into the game and eventually they won a free kick on the right-hand side of the box. Our defence in the wall stood tall as they were able to block the shot. Leeds continued to attack with all the team pressing, and although we won a couple of corners, were unable to make the pressure count. At one point when one of the Brentford players was down, another one had his arms around the referee. Klich had played well once again as Leeds were clapped off the pitch from an exuberant away support. It was a good point and they'd played well as a team and battled, which was good to see, and long may it continue. This will be our last visit to Griffin Park as Brentford move to their new ground shortly. In one sense, it is sad to see the demise of a traditional ground with terraces underneath the seating area for the away fans. Even though it hasn't been the best of grounds for us to win points over the years, it had a nice feel about it.

As Leeds showed today, a battling performance and being together with the fans are what we need going forwards. We've just got to believe and never give up and take each game as at comes. After a detour home, eventually getting to bed at 3am, I was up again at 6.30am for work along with lots of other Leeds fans. The things we do to follow our team! See you on Saturday against Bristol City. LUFC – Marching on Together!

LEEDS UNITED V BRISTOL CITY 15 FEBRUARY 2020 AT ELLAND ROAD

With other Leeds fans calling for our support to be the 12th man today, it was fantastic to see us getting that siege mentality back, getting behind the lads and having a fantastic atmosphere. We must do this for every game and it certainly made a difference today, along with a fighting performance from the team. Keep going Leeds, we can do this!

Despite storm Dennis on its way to lashing the UK today, I managed to get to Elland Road with my granddaughter Alexis during a lull in the weather. Getting there in good time, we went to the front of the club shop to meet Paul, who was buying two of my books Back to Reality and *Marcelo Bielsa's Leeds United*. Enjoy the read and it was good to hear that he enjoys reading my blogs all the time so thank you for the support. We had a quick visit to the Peacock, and it was nice to see some of the Halifax Whites in there with Shuy who was here from Australia. It turned out he had a ticket not far from me in the ground. Again, we timed it right getting into the ground before the rain started but it meant there would be challenging conditions for the players today.

Team: Casilla, Ayling, Cooper, White, Dallas, Costa, Bamford, Klich, Hernandez, Phillips and Harrison. Subs: Augustin for Bamford (75) and Shackleton for Hernandez (90). Leeds won the game 1-0, with a goal by Ayling (16). Attendance was 35,819, with 1,203 Bristol fans.

Leeds were up for the game from the off as we attacked towards the South Stand. We continued to attack and took a deserved lead in the 16th minute when Leeds had shot after shot blocked before Ayling got on the end of the ball to hit it into the net. Within a few minutes Bamford put the ball into the net to give us a second goal, or so we thought, only for the linesman to put his flag up for offside. Once again, a Bamford goal was chalked off by the officials. That is at least three goals he has been denied this season due to official decisions and one being awarded as an own goal instead. That is so frustrating for him and us. It felt like, had that goal been awarded, we would have gone on to get a hatful. Costa was brought down by a Bristol player, only for the referee to play on. With that Costa ran on and hit a fantastic shot that their keeper did well to save. I said he should get his angry head on more often! It had been a very one-sided game, with Leeds fighting for every ball, continuing to attack and keeping Bristol down to a late chance as we went into the break with a one-goal lead. The Leeds crowd had played their part too, which was great to see and hear despite many of them at the front of the stands having to contend with the worst of the weather. I'm glad our seats are far enough back and that we aren't in the family stand anymore as we used to get wet in those seats.

The second half saw Bristol attack first, but Leeds carried on dominating the game as Harrison and Costa kept attacking down the flanks. Phillips was in great form again, showing how much we had missed him as he put some great balls through. We looked dangerous every time we came forward and the Bristol keeper was in fantastic form as he kept out what looked like certain goals from Bamford and Costa. Bamford's shot was low and looked to be going under the keeper, only for him to land on the ball and stop it going into the goal. Costa had beaten the keeper, only for him to somehow fling himself at the ball to stop it going into the net. He led a charmed life that's for sure, and Bristol had him to thank for keeping the score down. As we had attack after attack, I thought we wouldn't attempt to make any changes to the team. I was disappointed to see Bamford was then taken off for Augustin as I didn't think he deserved to be subbed. What he brings to the team cannot be discounted and he looked disappointed to be taken off. I would like to have seen him stay on as well as Augustin as you could see immediately the difference once he went off. Shortly afterwards we gained the upper hand again as Harrison's shot hit the crossbar. We deserved that second goal but unfortunately with the woodwork and the keeper in outstanding form it was proving hard to get. We had limited Bristol to very few attacks and most of them were dealt with comfortably, although one looked too close for comfort. Shackleton came on to replace Hernandez to ensure we got the points. It was great to see Shackleton add pace to the game in injury time as Leeds attacked and we were unlucky that Augustin's shot went past the wrong side of the post.

As the final whistle blew, everyone on the terraces was ecstatic to get the win. As the cheering went on for ages it really was good to see how everyone had come together today and that is what we need to do every game. I loved this side today and everyone played their part so well done to everybody. The three points were particularly important today as we got the win and the bonus of a clean sheet as other teams around us capitulated. Another home game next week with Reading the visitors and hopefully I am meeting an Argentinian journalist so want to be there early. Enjoy the win everyone and see you next week. LUFC – Marching on Together!

LEEDS UNITED V READING 22 FEBRUARY 2020 AT ELLAND ROAD

Being back at Elland Road for the second home game in a week was just the therapy I needed after waking up not feeling well and having to drag myself to the game. Even though the trip was via Rastrick and Wakefield, as usual, once I was back at the ground and amongst our fans, I started to feel better. Whilst taking a photo of some friends, I had to encourage a Reading fan to join in for the photo. When he said I wouldn't want a Reading fan on the photo, my remark was that I don't discriminate against anyone and am very inclusive with my photos. With a quick trip to the Peacock, I hadn't realised there was a queue to the back door as I walked right past everyone until it was pointed out to me. It didn't take long to get in there though, and the Peacock choir were in full voice which was nice to hear. Going into the ground we went via the fan zone so we could hear Paul Wilson performing on the stage. His song The King of Elland Road was used to promote my book *Marcelo Bielsa's Leeds United* and my granddaughter Hannah loves singing this.

My walk to the front of the Kop took me to the right place where Argentinian journalist Andrea D'Emilio was just getting her photo taken. She had contacted me a few months back to say she was coming to the game and wanted to meet me. Thank you for a copy of the book she has written Los Locos Del Loco, La Hinchada de Marcelo Bielsa which is appreciated. She signed the book 'to Heidi a crazy Leeds fan' and I can guarantee that I certainly am lol!

Team: Casilla, Ayling, Cooper, White, Hernandez, Bamford, Costa, Klich, Phillips, Dallas and Harrison. Subs: Alioski for Phillips (injured 37) and Shackleton for Hernandez (85). Leeds won the game 1-0, with Hernandez scoring the Leeds goal (57). Attendance: 35,483, with 806 Reading fans.

With Leeds turned around at kick-off so that we would be attacking the Kop in the first half, for once I wasn't unduly worried or superstitious. As I said to someone before the game, I don't worry about any other club and make my observations on what I see on the pitch. With the weather conditions of heavy winds going to have an impact on the game, it was a case of playing the best we can. Leeds set off on the attack and Costa had a great chance that went wide of the post. After a foul on one of our players, the referee played the advantage and Klich brought a save out of their keeper. What was good to see was the referee then go back and book the player for the foul. The same thing had happened to Ayling previously when he ended up in the book after an advantage to Reading was played. Phillips made a couple of crunching tackles to win the ball as

Leeds continued to press forward. Casilla made a good save to keep Reading out just before the half-hour mark. Phillips was treated for an injury and sadly not long afterwards had to be replaced by Alioski. That was such a shame as he'd been playing well once again, but hopefully the injury isn't going to be too bad, although he was still limping at the end of the game. Dallas switched sides as Leeds reshuffled the team but continued to attack and were very unlucky to go into the break on equal terms due to good defending and goalkeeping. One attack had stood out when our player was in an offside position but stood back as another one took the ball forward. The linesman to our left immediately put his flag up as the Leeds fans were going mad saying the one offside hadn't touched the ball. I wasn't sure if the referee overruled him and we played on as I couldn't see to be sure, so hopefully someone else can clarify what happened.

Leeds started the second half on the attack too, coming close with shots from both Klich and Costa going wide. Bamford was the next to have a shot saved, before Leeds took the lead through Hernandez at the second attempt. With his first shot blocked, the ball rebounded for him to hit the ball into the top corner of the goal, to the delight of the Leeds United fans. Reading had been dealt with mostly as our players closed them down, but they won a free kick when their player was already on his way down before anyone touched him. Justice was served as their player blasted the ball way over the goal to the cheers of the Leeds fans. Hernandez's free kick brought a great save out of their keeper as we limited Reading's chances. In the last minutes of the game, though, Casilla made a great save to ensure we got the win right at the death. Another three points which is good to see in our challenge for automatic promotion. With two away games at both Boro and Hull, just play to our strengths and don't give up. We can do this Leeds! See you there, LUFC – Marching on Together!

MIDDLESBROUGH V LEEDS UNITED 26 FEBRUARY 2020 AT THE RIVERSIDE

Travelling to the game after work, I found out on the coach that I'd won a corporate ticket to the Huddersfield game. As someone who always wears my Leeds colours, it was a relief to know that I can still do that. Having never been in corporate before as I prefer to be on the terraces, it will be a different experience that's for sure. I'm going to meet a friend for my book *Marcelo Bielsa's Leeds United* a bit earlier than intended now, so hopefully that doesn't impact too much on her. Also, it was nice to see Jonny Joseph, secretary of LUSC Los Angeles, travelling with us to the game.

We were the last coach to arrive for the police escort and we set off as soon as we got there. Getting to the ground was no issue but trying to get 15 coachloads of Leeds fans who arrived at the same time through the turnstiles was a bigger challenge. I met some Leeds fans who said they'd been talking to a friend in Australia who knew me. As I share my blog with the Australian Whites it is nice to know that fans do read it. Another fan told me to keep posting on LinkedIn too so thank you everyone who does read my blogs. Eventually, as one of the queues didn't move, I went through a different one but only one turnstile was working. Eventually the second one started working again but then the lad in front of me couldn't get his ticket to work. At first we thought it was because we were in the wrong turnstile according to the ticket, but he let me through first and mine worked. Luckily, we still got in before kick-off and my flag was put up at the front of the stand. I went the wrong way across the stand to find my seat before I retraced my steps and found it just as the game started. I also had to delete lots of photos on my camera as the SD card was full, what an idiot for not checking it from Saturday! It meant I had to go back at the end of the game to find our steward Phil 'Thumbsup' Cresswell who was celebrating his 60th birthday, as the photo I took at the start wouldn't open.

Team: Casilla, Ayling, Cooper, White, Berardi, Hernandez, Bamford, Costa, Harrison, Klich and Dallas. Sub: Shackleton for Hernandez (73). Leeds won the game with a goal by Klich in injury time at the end of the first half (45+1). Attendance: 24,647, with 4,400 Leeds fans.

It didn't take long to realise that Boro's finishing was very poor and I felt that the game was there for the taking. Even though we weren't passing brilliantly at times, which went to Boro players instead, their shots at goal were way off target, with one going out for a Leeds throw. As far as I was concerned, they could do that all game. One thing I noticed was they had narrowed the pitch, which I felt took us a little while to get used to. We'd had a couple of chances with a Bamford header being saved and another shot from him going narrowly wide. Stuart Dallas had a great shot saved by their keeper before we had a penalty appeal turned down when Costa was brought down in the area. Leeds continued to attack and both Harrison and Bamford had shots saved by their keeper. With injury time on the clock, Leeds pressed forward again, and Bamford passed the ball to Hernandez, only to see his shot bounce back off the post. Just when we thought the chance had gone, Hernandez got the ball again and passed to Klich, who put the ball into the net to send the Leeds fans wild just before the whistle went for half-time. A very timely goal to put us in a good position. There was a lively atmosphere down underneath the stands, which wasn't surprising but it's nice to hear happy singing Leeds fans.

The second half saw the Boro keeper once again keeping a Leeds shot out, this time from Dallas. Not long after this, Boro looked as if they wanted to get something out of the game and Casilla was called into action, making a great save from a long-range shot. They started to put some pressure on us but our breaking out from defence into attack was good to see. The keeper then denied Hernandez a goal before we had another penalty appeal turned down. This one was even more blatant when Harrison was fouled in the area, but the referee played on. He did play on numerous times for both sides, which is better than having stop-and-start free kicks all over the place, but he got that decision wrong. Harrison was limping for a short while afterwards. I thought Howson started to get into the game more, which impacted on the way Boro played and they hit the crossbar with Casilla beaten. That was the only time I worried they may get back into the game. Leeds looked certain to double the lead as Ayling passed the ball from the byline across

the goalmouth. As shouts went up saying how did Bamford miss that one, replays later showed that the ball deflected just in front of him, which luckily for Boro ensured their keeper could save it. The deflection was the difference that meant the ball didn't go into the net. I said it wasn't going to make a difference as we would win, Boro were rubbish and weren't allowed to score. We didn't give up and Harrison came close again with another shot going narrowly wide. Leeds had to be on their toes in the final minutes when Boro won a free kick just outside the area, with Casilla eventually saving the ball after a deflection. We managed to see the game out to get a vital win and another three points. That'll do for me Leeds, so keep going! After the team had clapped the Leeds fans at the end of the game, Phillips, who was still injured, came and got the Leeds fans cheering three times with his new routine again. As the team were heading off the pitch, suddenly the few Boro fans behind the goal started trying to get to some Leeds fans. When I zoomed the camera in, they were mostly young kids, oh dear!

Saturday sees us head to Hull for the lunchtime kick-off but same as Boro tonight, the clubs could have given us even more tickets and we would have sold them. I can't believe they would rather throw the money away than have Leeds fans take over their grounds even more! With more bad weather forecast for the weekend with high winds, I hope they shut the high bridge at Goole as I do not want to go over that. I can remember going over there in a double decker bus with the Halifax Whites and many of them on the top deck were trying to get the bus to tip over by all going to the seats at the left-hand side. To say I was worried is an understatement. It was that same horrendous feeling I'd had whilst crossing Carlton Bridge last Sunday with the river high and starting to flood, which two days later became a torrent. See you on Saturday, LUFC – Marching on Together!

HULL CITY V LEEDS UNITED 29 FEBRUARY 2020 AT THE KCOM STADIUM

Leeds United are never out of the news, but the timing of the FA revealing their results from the Kiko case showed their true colours once again. The announcement at 7.30pm the evening before our game today proclaimed they had found him guilty on the probability of his supposed racist comment when we played at Charlton last year. Why on earth were their written findings not announced too so they could be scrutinised to see how they came to that conclusion? What happened to innocent until proven guilty? Why is it assumed that the accuser was telling the truth and not Kiko when he denied the accusations? I think it is disgraceful that when Kiko said he would never use words in a racist meaning the FA are able to cast a slur on someone that will be there for the rest of his life with their decision. I never saw anything untoward happen during the Charlton game and didn't capture any photos that I took at the time that would have said something had taken place. Kiko had the support of the Leeds fans at the game today, which shows that I'm not the only one questioning the decision that was made. I await the written findings from the FA now.

Our morning stop was in Selby and back in my neck of the woods. My friend Sue and I met at

Selby High for Girls in 1966 and have been friends ever since. Her dad took me to my first Leeds game for Sue's 12th birthday and, as you say, the rest is history as we are still here supporting our team. By the time we arrived in Hull the sun was shining. With more storms on the horizon it was a nice surprise. This time we had been given behind the goal which had sold out in minutes, but I know many Leeds fans had their tickets cancelled in the Hull end in the last few days. With an empty upper tier in the main stand, it would have made sense to sell them to our fans as they'd have sold out quickly too. The Leeds fans were in good voice underneath the stand where I'd gone after putting my flag up. With lads on shoulders or balancing on the partitions, they were keeping the rest of us entertained. I'd been queuing for a cuppa only to realise it was five minutes to kick-off so abandoned my queue to go to my seat.

Team: Meslier, Cooper, Ayling, White, Hernandez, Harrison, Costa, Bamford, Dallas, Phillips and Klich. Subs: Roberts for Bamford (66), Shackleton for Hernandez (88) and Alioski for Harrison (89). Leeds won the game 4-0 with goals from Ayling (5), Hernandez (47) and Roberts with a brace (81 and 84). Attendance was 16,178, with 3,519 Leeds fans plus 100+ in the Hull ends who came to join us in the away end.

With a Leeds United team and the fans having a siege mentality today, we had to show others that together we are a force to be reckoned with. Within five minutes we got off to a flying start, taking the lead when a fantastic shot from outside the area hurtled into the net from a deflection. As I was wondering who number seven was because I didn't have my glasses on, the fans starting chanting for Ayling. I must have had reminisces of Peter Lorimer with that shot. As the sun was shining so brightly and it was hard to see, I put my glasses on as they have tinted lenses. It also got very hot in the sun, although later when it went behind the clouds there was a chill in the air. A few minutes later another fantastic shot from Hernandez bounced back off the crossbar when it looked destined to give us a second goal. With Meslier making his league debut, he was very composed, having taken the place of Casilla, and I felt we were in safe hands. He made a save from a deflected Hull shot but Hull didn't really put him under too much pressure. We had lots of possession during the first half and when Phillips was bundled off the ball to set up a Hull attack, he looked very upset. I think it was Ayling who tried to cheer him up. With Phillips coming back in after his injury, it looked like he may have to go off at half-time as Berardi was being warmed up at the side of the pitch. Both Harrison and Costa were playing well down both wings, but we weren't able to capitalise on our dominance before the break.

Luckily for us, Phillips came back out for the second half as we set off with a bang after Hull had an early chance to equalise. Meslier made the save and a minute later we had doubled our lead. A great cross from Harrison saw Costa pass the ball to Hernandez, who stuck it into the net to the jubilance of the Leeds fans. As Leeds continued to dominate, Hull had their keeper to thank for keeping our score down to two goals as he saved from both Costa and Klich. Hull did have a couple of chances but Meslier was on form, tipping the ball over the crossbar, and with another I thought

he'd pushed the ball around the post when in fact it had hit it. He had the ball covered though. Bamford was booked after he'd been fouled. He'd got around their player on the wing after being held back and then their player pushed Bamford right in front of the referee. We couldn't believe both getting booked instead of just the Hull player. Harrison hit a great shot which bounced back off the post with the keeper beaten, which was a shame as he deserved a goal for that effort. When Costa had another shot saved by the keeper, Hull should be thankful he kept the score line down. As it was, we did increase our lead, with Roberts getting a brace after pinpoint passes from Klich. The first was after Leeds charged out from defence with some great attacking, which Roberts finished off, and the second one was a header. That was it, game over as Hull fans streamed to the exits with the Leeds fans celebrating. The result was no more than we deserved though, and it was so nice to get a big win and the just rewards for our dominance even though at times it wasn't a good game. In the last 15 minutes though, our fitness levels told, as we were charging out of defence. I thought Harrison played very well today, and Costa got into the game a lot too. That was the reply needed from Leeds today to the powers that be, and long may it continue. On our way out of the ground there were a group of fans here from Argentina and one of them took a photo including me and then I caught our rogue's gallery of stewards going back to the coaches. On our way back to Leeds a couple of photos showed how bad the flooding was in my locality, which was sad to see.

Next week sees me going in early for my hospitality win, but I may still go in my own seat for the game. I need to meet up with some fans and catch some of the Peacock Choir singing prior to the game so as usual it will be a busy day. Thanks for the feedback today from fans who have read my books, blogs or who want to meet up for signings. As always, your comments are appreciated. See you on Saturday, LUFC – Marching on Together!

CHAPTER 9 – MARCH AND APRIL 2020

LEEDS UNITED V HUDDERSFIELD TOWN 7 MARCH 2020 AT ELLAND ROAD

I'd not been worried at all about today's game until a lad started talking to me about it at work. Suddenly, my stomach churning started but I decided that my out of sight, out of mind method works best! Just concentrate on Leeds United, it works wonders. Having been ill all week which I've blamed on going to Hull, it meant I haven't posted as much this week. As we headed to Elland Road earlier than usual, it was because I'd won a couple of corporate tickets for the game. It was going to be a change to my usual routine of heading to the Peacock as my hubby accompanied me into the Pavilion. The place was packed out with more tables than usual, and I know for some fans it is the only way they can get a ticket now Elland Road is sold out every game. We enjoyed a three-course meal, drinks (we stuck with water and soft drinks) and saw Jermaine Beckford, Tony Dorigo, John Hendrie, Steve Hodge and Neil Aspin. The latter remembered coming to the Selby branch of the supporter's club do when he won player of the year, which he said must have been in 1985. Ian and his daughter Lucy from Stafford had got the other pair of tickets in our group who also enjoyed the great hospitality that had been put on. The staff were very helpful and there was a good atmosphere in there. There were fans who had travelled from Bulgaria, Thailand, Australia and later I met a Danish Leeds fan, to name a few, which shows once again the great worldwide fanbase we have.

Thank you for the support Tina, who had travelled from Scotland for the game, for buying my book *Marcelo Bielsa's Leeds United*. Also, thanks to those of you who spoke to me about following my blogs too. As we headed into the game, things didn't quite go to plan. I was swapping places with my daughter Michelle as she was joining my hubby in the corporate seats, whilst I was going in the Kop as usual with my daughter Danielle and granddaughter Laura. As I waited for the girls, my hubby was queuing to get into the stand only to come back out of the turnstile. The damn ticket wouldn't work, and it turns out that his wasn't the only ticket with an issue today. As it was close to kick-off, we got him in on the other ticket to make sure that one worked, and Michelle went to get a new one printed. We got in just before the teams came out.

Team: Meslier, Ayling, Cooper, Berardi, White, Dallas, Harrison, Costa, Bamford, Hernandez and Klich. Subs: Roberts for Bamford (79), Shackleton for Klich (83) and Alioski for Harrison (90). Leeds won the game 2-0 with goals from Luke Ayling (3) and Bamford (51). Attendance was 36,514, with 2,647 Town fans, who'd sold out their allocation, making this the highest of the season.

With Phillips out injured, Berardi came back into the defence again, with White taking Phillips's role. Leeds got off to a thunderous start, taking the lead in the third minute. Harrison

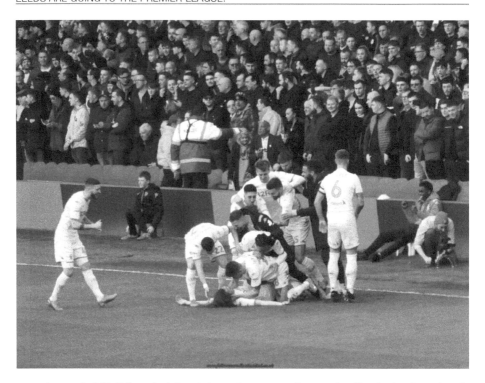

crossed a wonderful ball from the left to Ayling, who met it with a superb volley that hit the underside of the crossbar before hitting the back of the net as Elland Road erupted. What a start, that is just what we needed to set the tone of the game. I'd say that was a great celebration from Ayling for his daughter's third birthday today. Things evened out for a while as Town had a good chance, but Meslier managed to save the ball when he sat on it. They had a couple of corners and had lots of players trying to put Meslier off, and it was nice to end up with the free kick for a foul with one of them.

Before the game when scores were being predicted, nearly everyone said we would concede one goal, whereas I insisted we had to give them nothing. Our breaking out of defence into attack nearly brought us a second goal, but Costa's chance went wide, as did another couple of chances by Harrison and White.

We'd gone into the break in the lead and I said we needed to start the second half the same as we did the first. Well I wasn't far wrong. Although their keeper had to be on his toes to keep out both Harrison and Bamford, we increased our lead six minutes after the restart. Leeds won a free kick to the left of the box, which Hernandez took. Their keeper made a fantastic save from White, but Bamford made no mistake when the ball came to him and he stuck it into the net to lift the roof off Elland Road. I was pleased to see Bamford get the just rewards for his hard work of recent weeks. During the game we were guilty of some bad passing at times from Berardi and Hernandez, which resulted in Town getting the upper hand, but overall we managed to deal with them quite well. When Harrison hit a fantastic shot from the left of us, it hit the angle of the crossbar and post to the right of us and Hernandez's shot was then blocked. Wow, that move so deserved a goal. Elland Road was bouncing as the noise erupted around the ground into fever pitch as Leeds played some fantastic passing football. This was brought to a halt when a Town player went down before going off injured. That was a real shame because it took the sting out of the game. Although Town hadn't given up when one shot rebounded off Meslier, our defence were there backing him up and got the ball to safety. When the linesman to our left went off injured and the fourth official came on instead, we were hoping that he'd be better with the offside rule. Wrong! The first thing he did was put the flag up for offside to a chorus of boos from the Leeds fans. I hadn't been unduly worried about them scoring but knew we'd be heading into a lot of injury time. With the goal, all the subs and the referee injury, I was expecting at least seven minutes added on, so it was a nice surprise to see only five minutes on the clock. When their player went down in the penalty area under a challenge in front of the South Stand, my heart sank as I expected the referee to point to the penalty spot. It was a relief when he gave a goal kick, and someone said their player was booked for diving. The referee had been very busy with his bookings today with three Leeds and three Town in total going into the book.

Another win and another three points, which is all I ask for. Well done Leeds United as you've sent a fan base home very happy. Don't worry about those other teams around us, concentrate on us and play to our strengths. We can do this, just keep fighting and never give up. See you for that early start to Cardiff on Sunday, LUFC – Marching on Together!

Thank you to Zion Digital for becoming the Official *Follow Me and Leeds United* website sponsor for 2019/20, www.followmeandleedsunited.co.uk.

Zion Digital provide Digital Marketing services such as websites, SEO, email, e-commerce and many others, to get your business online, and to get it seen.

We're in Halifax but cover the whole of the UK and internationally, working with global partners such as Google, Microsoft, Amazon and many more to improve brands and increase your online profile.

Special offer for Leeds fans 20% off mentioning 'BIELSA' on 03300 43 1968 or email us at LUFC@zion.digital until the end of this 'hopefully' glorious season! OnOnOn!

CORONAVIRUS – ALL THE FOLLOWING GAMES ARE POSTPONED: CARDIFF A, FULHAM H, LUTON H, BAYERN MUNICH, BLACKBURN A, STOKE CITY H, SWANSEA A, BARNSLEY H, DERBY A AND CHARLTON H

Having had time to get my head around the football season grinding to a halt because of the Coronavirus outbreak, who knows what is going to happen next. The world we take for granted has changed beyond recognition with everything shutting down for many of us. I found it very tough at first and admit I cried on Monday, 23 March when the reality set in with Boris's announcement that we were in lockdown as a country. Having a close family and knowing I can't see my grandchildren, kids and my mum had me in bits.

To try and take my mind off things and to help in a positive way, I decided to share photos I have taken over the years at Leeds United games. This has had a positive impact amongst our fans, bringing back many memories, with my post on the WACCOE forum having over 16,000 views.

When the league stopped on 13 March 2020 due to coronavirus, the top six and bottom three in the table were:

POS	TEAM	P	W	D	L	F	A	GD	PTS
1	LEEDS UNITED	37	21	8	8	56	30	26	**71**
2	WEST BROMWICH ALBION	37	19	13	5	64	37	27	70
3	FULHAM	37	18	10	9	52	38	14	64
4	BRENTFORD	37	17	9	11	64	33	31	60
5	NOTTINGHAM FOREST	37	16	12	9	48	38	10	60
6	PRESTON	37	16	8	13	50	45	5	56
22	CHARLTON ATHLETIC	37	10	9	18	44	54	-10	39
23	LUTON TOWN	37	10	5	22	43	71	-28	35
24	BARNSLEY	37	8	10	19	42	62	-20	34

Hearing first that Norman Hunter had died and then two weeks later Trevor Cherry had died too was devastating for the Leeds United support.

Firstly, 17 April 2020 saw the sad news that our Leeds United legend Norman Hunter had died of Coronavirus. Norman was part of the team who gave me the best years of my life following Leeds United and I salute you.

Then Trevor Cherry on 29 April 2020. You were always my friend Carole's hero, hence why she made her banner, Power to yer boot Trevor. More sad news and so soon after losing Norman Hunter.

Thoughts with both of their families and friends at these sad times. Plenty of tears were shed but it helped sharing photos and talking about both of them on social media. Also, with my friends Margaret, Sue, Paul, Carole and Ashley, we raised a toast to Norman and Trevor.

Rest in Peace Norman and Trevor, you will never be forgotten.

CHAPTER 10 – JUNE 2020

Football restarts for Leeds United at Cardiff City on 21 June 2020 at the Cardiff City Stadium but behind closed doors with no fans allowed!

Surreal times today as the season carries on where it left off in March with the first of nine outstanding games being played. We start with the visit to Cardiff but for the first time ever, all these games are to be played behind closed doors. Fans who have had unbroken runs of games over many years with some from the 60s onwards were not allowed to travel to any games. This decision was gutting and, from a personal point of view, I prefer to be watching a game live at the ground rather than watching it on TV.

Team: Meslier, Ayling, White, Cooper, Dallas, Phillips, Costa, Roberts, Klich, Harrison and Bamford. Subs: Alioski for Ayling (62), Ian Poveda (making his debut) for Costa (77) and Robbie Gotts making his league debut for Klich (84). Leeds lost the game 2-0. Attendance was zero – behind closed doors.

The team looking slim and fit after weeks in lockdown was good to see. I thought White looked nervy to begin with, but he grew into the game and an innocuous challenge with him saw a Cardiff player go down like a sack of spuds. Cardiff were the stronger of the two teams in the opening 15 minutes, before Leeds looked to get a grip of the game. We were having more possession and came close when Dallas crossed the ball to the far post and Ayling's header brought a save out of the keeper. Although Leeds were playing some good movements going forwards, I felt we were trying to walk the ball into the net too often. There was too much pussy footing around in the penalty area with not enough power on passes, enabling Cardiff to clear the ball with ease. I wanted Leeds to shoot from outside the area, which we started to do during our good run before the enforced break, as this would catch Cardiff unawares. When they were packing everyone into their defence it was always going to be difficult to break them down. The new rule of a water break didn't go down well with me as it stopped the momentum of the game. Leeds were looking comfortable as the ball ended up with Phillips in our half. He casually passed the ball without looking where he was putting it, only to see the Cardiff player accept the misplaced pass. With that, Cardiff were on the attack and a minute later took a lead against the run of play. A great shot from outside the area beat Meslier at the top of the near post. Just before half-time Leeds came very close to an equaliser when Harrison hit the ball at the goal but straight at Bamford who was in front of him. Sadly, their keeper got the ball before it could be put into the net. Although frustrating, it wouldn't have counted anyway as the linesman put the offside flag up. There were two more times during the game when the flag was put up wrongly, as replays showed that Leeds were not offside for either of those moves. It was frustrating to go in a goal down at half-time.

Leeds came out attacking at the start of the second period, with Costa putting a great ball across the box but just out of reach of both Bamford and Harrison. It was a good move though. Their keeper made a great point-blank save from Roberts to deny Leeds an equaliser after Bamford's header gave him a great opportunity. Cardiff then took a further lead after another mistake, this time from Cooper. His ball out to the wing was intercepted by their player, who ran towards goal and hit an unstoppable shot past Meslier with the help of a post. That made our job of getting something out of this game even harder. A couple of chances for Dallas and Alioski went over the bar. Phillips nearly made us pay again with a quick free kick that saw Klich under pressure immediately as the Cardiff player tried to intercept the ball. This saw Klich booked, as he had to stop their player from going through as there would have been no one else to beat but the keeper. That was a stupid ball to give in the first place and I felt we were being too complacent at times. Gotts came on as a sub, followed by Poveda, both making their debuts, but Leeds were unable to get anything out of the game as we went down to a loss at Cardiff. We never seem to do well here, but also Neil Harris their manager always seems to be able to get one over us. If the game had been played when it should before lockdown, I felt we'd have got something out of the game then, with the momentum we had built up.

We now have a week's rest before we play Fulham for our first home game next Saturday, again behind closed doors. It's not the end of the world Leeds, so just keep fighting. You've got the 15,000 'Crowdies' behind you together with some Leeds singing that has been put together. We'll all be cheering you on from afar so get the win and three points for us please.

LEEDS UNITED V FULHAM 27 JUNE 2020 AT ELLAND ROAD

With our first home game behind closed doors, being at home instead of at the game is taking its toll. My stomach churning went into overdrive, but I wanted an early goal to settle the nerves. It has made me realise that the distraction of taking photos at games certainly helps to keep me more focussed. I'd like to say well done to members of the WACCOE forum for their new banner in the Norman Hunter South Stand for both Norman and Trevor Cherry. It looks fantastic and is a great tribute to both players, who will be sadly missed.

Team: Meslier, Ayling, Dallas, Cooper, White, Phillips, Klich (making his 100th appearance), Bamford, Roberts, Costa and Harrison. Subs: Alioski for Costa (45), Hernandez for Bamford (45), Douglas for Klich (80), Poveda for Harrison (83) and Shackleton for Hernandez (90+2). Leeds won the game 3-0, with goals from Bamford (10), Alioski (56) and Harrison (71). Attendance was 15,000 crowdies and played behind closed doors.

In the opening two minutes, Fulham should have been reduced to ten men after a deliberate elbow from Mitrovic. With none of the officials seeing the incident or acting on it, retrospective action needs to be taken by the powers that be. Watch this space … There was another incident on Roberts where he kept the ball in between his knees, only to end up being studded across his knee by another Fulham player. To me it was already obvious that Fulham were ready to rough us up

and put us off our game. Within ten minutes, though, Bamford put Leeds ahead after some great work from Costa, who passed the ball into the middle for him to put a first-time shot into the goal. That was what I ordered to relieve the nerves! After we scored, Fulham had the most possession and Meslier was called into action with two saves from powerful shots. Fulham also thought they should have had a penalty for hand ball. Despite all their possession, Fulham couldn't capitalise on it and we nearly scored a second right on the break when Bamford beat the keeper, only for the ball to go agonisingly wide. We hadn't played our usual football in the first half. We were clearing the ball by kicking it away rather than playing it away, but it was more to do with keeping Fulham out, despite them having most of the play.

It was no surprise to see that Bielsa had made changes in the second half – Hernandez and Alioski coming on for Bamford and Costa with Roberts going up front. Our passing and movement became crisper as we got the better of Fulham and came close to scoring when Harrison's shot was deflected wide after Klich had sent a great pass for Roberts to run onto. Meslier pushed a free kick over the bar but from their corner Leeds took advantage with a great counter-attack to score a second goal. Harrison's great run down the wing saw his ball across the box come to Alioski, who fired it home and went to celebrate with the crowdies behind the goal. That was just what we needed to get on top in the game and it put a little bit of a distance between us and Fulham. Meslier was called into action again, but not long after another fantastic move saw Hernandez put a great pass across to Harrison, who took the ball all the way and slotted it past their keeper for a third goal. The momentum took Harrison into the crowdies too to celebrate. It was great seeing the game go our way and Fulham sent on their way. After the lapses of the referee in booking Mitrovic and the one who studded our player earlier in the game, he made up for it in the second half. He gave a Fulham player a second booking in the 90th minute to send him off. The game ended in torrential rain and with five substitutes allowed (although still over three stoppages), Shackleton was brought on for Hernandez, which I felt was Bielsa looking after him. I love Alioski; seeing him going around the pitch at the end of the game clapping the crowdies was brilliant.

A good win and three points took Leeds back to the top of the table as West Bromwich Albion lost yesterday to Brentford. With seven games left, we have a midweek home game against Luton Town on Tuesday and Blackburn away on Saturday so keep the momentum going Leeds, we are all behind you. LUFC – Marching on Together!

LEEDS UNITED V LUTON TOWN 30 JUNE 2020 AT ELLAND ROAD

I had no idea where Luton were in the table until just before the game, and I'd rather have not known as it always puts extra pressure on us.

Team: Meslier, Cooper, Dallas, White, Ayling, Phillips, Costa, Roberts, Bamford, Klich and Harrison. Subs: Berardi for Cooper (injured 12), Alioski for Berardi (45), Hernandez for Klich (61) and Shackleton for Dallas (injured 90+4). We drew 1-1 with Dallas getting an equaliser (63).

Attendance was 15,000 crowdies and played behind closed doors.

Luton had a man booked for a foul on Dallas in the first few minutes. The first half on the whole was like watching paint dry as I was ready to fall asleep at times. We lost Liam Cooper to an injury and Berardi was brought on to replace him in the early stages of the game. Leeds found Luton crowding round our players giving them no room to move, meaning we couldn't break them down, plus we had a lot of misplaced passes. As it was, Luton came the closest to scoring when Meslier made a good save to prevent it. We ended the half with corner after corner but what a disaster the first three were as each one was sent nearly back to the half-way line and we lost any impetus from having a corner. The ones following were better, but we couldn't take any advantage from them, although Klich brought a save from their keeper after one of them. The differences in our corners to the way Luton did them are that we don't crowd their keeper and have no one on the goal line. The thing is, though, when we are struggling to get near the goal to have a shot, not getting the ball into the area from the number of corners we had was a waste. All in all, it was a frustrating game so far.

At the start of the second half Alioski had come on for Berardi as we changed formation to three at the back. Alioski was making some runs down the left wing as we started brighter and looked livelier. Against the run of play though, Luton scored. They got the ball and, with White marking him in the penalty area, I was expecting him to cross to another player, but he shot, and it went straight into the net. Leeds immediately started to put more pressure on Luton as we started opening them up more. Bamford's shot deflected wide, then Harrison and Roberts brought a save out of their keeper. Their keeper was being kept busy, saving from a Phillip's free kick and another shot from Costa. When Hernandez came on, we started moving even better and eventually, after a great move with Alioski running down the wing, he sent a great ball into the middle for Dallas to put the ball into the net to equalise. Meslier came running out of goal to head the ball away from a Luton player as they counter-attacked, but that was a little close for comfort. Their player was booked for a foul on Meslier though, who was holding his side. Alioski again crossed a great ball which went agonisingly wide from Bamford. Harrison put a great ball over for Bamford and it looked like he was going to head it into the goal, only for him to miss it completely. Costa did the same later in the game. Later, they both mentioned issues with the lights or maybe they took their eyes off the ball. Dallas brought another save from their keeper and had another shot deflect wide. Dallas put one shot over the bar, but I saw him hold on to the back of his leg. He kept limping and ended up going off, with Shackleton replacing him in injury time. Ayling was denied by their keeper as the game ended in a draw. I said it wasn't an ideal thing if we drew, but we could not lose the game. We did have a few chances, but their keeper was in the right place to keep us out.

I was only glad we didn't lose the game as we need every point to count. To me, the first half where we let them dictate the game proved to be costly for us. With WBA going back to the top midweek and Charlton challenging, it is going to be very tight. We must win at Blackburn on Saturday.

CHAPTER 11 – JULY 2020

BLACKBURN ROVERS V LEEDS UNITED 4 JULY 2020 AT EWOOD PARK

I dreamt that I was trying my hardest to get to the game without success, then I woke up. Although I was at Newcastle rather than Blackburn, it shows that I desperately want to be back at games watching Leeds live rather than being at home watching on TV. Sadly, no one knows when that will be.

Team: Meslier, Ayling, Cooper, White, Douglas, Klich, Phillips, Alioski, Roberts, Harrison and Bamford. Subs: Hernandez for Roberts (61) and Shackleton for Klich (89). Bamford (7), Phillips (40) and Klich (53) were the scorers for Leeds in a 3-1 away win. Attendance was zero – behind closed doors.

With two changes to the team with Douglas in for Dallas and Alioski in for Costa, who are both injured, I felt that was a good line up. The first few minutes were quite even before Bamford was sent a great through ball from Klich, who had robbed their player of possession and struck the ball low into the net to give us an early lead. Brilliant, that is just what we needed. We nearly succumbed to an equaliser straight away though when their player ran through the middle of our back line and hit the ball low. I thought it had gone straight into the net, but luckily for us it went past the wrong side of the post. We then started messing about at the back with the ball and inviting Blackburn to attack us. Again, they got through and luckily the ball hit the post and came out and we cleared it. At this point I was screaming at us to stop messing about at the back and play to our strengths. Luckily for us, we did settle down more and started to play. There was plenty of play from both sides as the game continued with end-to-end football. One of the Blackburn players went down injured and there was a break in play in the wet conditions. The ball was holding up at times on the wet ground and the ball had to be changed at one time as it was under deflated. Bamford had another chance that hit the post. Leeds won a couple of corners and first Phillips took one, which was sent into the middle. The second one was taken by Douglas and Leeds were unlucky when Ayling's low shot was saved on the line by their keeper. Leeds won a free kick at the edge of the area after a foul on Roberts. As we tried working out who was going to take it between Phillips, Douglas and Harrison, Phillips stepped up to hit a fantastic shot over the keeper and into the top corner of the net to give us a two-goal cushion. This was the score at half-time, and it was a good feeling knowing we had got that lead going into the second half. Keep it up Leeds, keep fighting!

Within three minutes of the start, Blackburn had pulled a goal back. They won a free kick when Phillips didn't jump for the ball and was adjudged to have fouled their player. From the resulting free kick, the ball went over the wall into the top right-hard corner of the goal with Meslier not moving. The replay showed that he didn't stand a chance of getting anywhere near it. Someone posted afterwards about him being too far to the far side of the goal, leaving the wall to cover the other side, which suggested to me that this is something all our keepers are being told to do. This is something that stood out for me when Casilla was in goal but all it does is invite the opposition to score in the big space in front of them. It was a good goal from a free kick though, sadly. Although Blackburn pulling a goal back so soon wasn't good, Leeds didn't let it deter them. We attacked again, coming close to an equaliser before we did get that two-goal cushion again in the 53rd minute. When the ball rebounded to Klich on the edge of the box, he hit a low shot into the net. Apparently it was a deflection, but I'd have to look at it again. As long as it goes into the net, that is all that matters. With another attack, Bamford was clean through after another good pass from Klich and was brought down by their keeper just outside the box. Instead of getting a straight red for being the last man, he escaped with a yellow card and then saved the free kick from Douglas. Leeds kept the lead, got the win and the three points to keep their automatic promotion hopes alive. Onto Stoke at home next Thursday with five games remaining.

LEEDS UNITED V STOKE CITY 9 JULY 2020 AT ELLAND ROAD

It's been a busy week for me starting with a live interview shown on Facebook on Monday, 6 July with LUFCnews.co.uk. I didn't even realise the interview was going to be live until I logged on to the Zoom meeting, but it stopped me getting nervous beforehand. With being able to talk a lot, at least, it went very well, and I thank them for the opportunity. Tomorrow sees a film crew coming to my garden for a socially distanced interview for Danz Brazil who are doing a piece on Marcelo Bielsa. Then before the game today, a piece I had done for the Leeds United Trust, asking fans to support the team from afar, was aired alongside ones from Adam Pope and Paul Trevillion.

From early morning I had severe butterflies before the game but was adamant we have to concentrate on ourselves and play to our strengths. Forget about the chasing pack which sadly, once again, has ended up with three teams vying for that automatic promotion. Getting so stressed before the game, trying to log onto a web meeting without success, proved to work for me in one sense as it kept the nerves away. I know I'm not the only one who is nervous as so much is riding on promotion again this season.

Team: Meslier, Dallas (back from injury), Cooper, White, Harrison, Costa (back from injury), Ayling, Phillips, Klich, Roberts and Bamford. Subs: Hernandez for Roberts (45), Douglas for Dallas (75), Shackleton for Klich (78) and Alioski for Harrison (78). Leeds won the game 5-0 with goals from a Klich penalty (45), Costa (47), Cooper (57), Hernandez (72) and Bamford (90+3). Attendance was 15,000 crowdies – played behind closed doors.

Leeds United put on a fantastic performance to ensure they went back to the top of the Championship table. Leeds had the first attack of the game, bringing a save out of their keeper from Roberts. Stoke were given a free kick outside the penalty area which went wide with a deflected shot. That was more or less the nearest they came to scoring, as Leeds were gaining possession and started attacking more. We were then denied a goal when first Bamford's shot had a goal line clearance and Roberts followed up only to see the same thing happen to him. Despite all our possession, it looked as if Stoke were going to keep the score level, only for Costa to be brought down at the edge of the penalty area right on half-time. Klich stepped up to coolly slot the ball into the right-hand side of the net to give us a deserved lead.

Hernandez came on at the start of the second half and within a couple of minutes Costa got the better of the defender and hit a shot past their keeper to double our lead. That gave us some breathing space. Bamford was unlucky once again when he hit the crossbar, but it wasn't long before we got a third goal when Cooper's shot went in off the post. Stoke were being completely outplayed and weren't even in the game, such was the domination of Leeds. They did have one attack but Leeds straight away counter-attacked, with their keeper making a save from Harrison. To cap it all, first Hernandez scored and then Bamford scored another in the dying minutes to give Leeds a fantastic 5-0 win on the night. On another day Bamford could have had a hat-trick save for the crossbar and the goal-line clearance. Any more thoughts of nervousness had been diminished very quickly for the Leeds team as their confidence grew. With an away game at Swansea next, the final positions in the league look to be going down to the final game. Keep fighting Leeds, you can do it!

10 JULY 2020 – RIP JACK CHARLTON

On Saturday, 11 July, Leeds fans once again woke up to the sad news that another of Revie's legends, Jack Charlton, had died peacefully at home yesterday after a long illness. Again, the news caused tears to fall freely, as another one of the players who was part of the greatest football team

I had the privilege to see joins our football team in heaven. Three legends have now died in the last three months with first Norman Hunter and then Trevor Cherry. Thank you for all those cherished memories. Rest in Peace big Jack, you will never be forgotten. Thoughts with your family and friends at this sad time.

SWANSEA CITY 12 JULY 2020 AT THE LIBERTY STADIUM

After the sad news about Jack Charlton yesterday, the Leeds team came out for training wearing t-shirts with Rip Big Jack on them. There was also a minute's silence in his honour. I was honoured to pay my respects live on TV when ITV did a tribute programme to him the following day.

Team: Meslier, Ayling, Cooper, White, Dallas, Klich, Harrison, Costa, Roberts, Phillips and Bamford. Subs: Alioski for Dallas (45), Hernandez for Roberts (45), Shackleton for Costa (90+3) and Berardi for Harrison (90+6). Leeds won the game 1-0, with a goal by Hernandez in the 89th minute. Attendance was zero – behind closed doors.

Swansea had the first chance in the game, which Meslier saved. Swansea had a couple more attacks, but Leeds were very unlucky not to take the lead on the half-hour mark when Bamford's shot was saved by their keeper. He also made a save from Costa just before the break.

Alioski and Hernandez came on at the start of the second half as Bielsa tried to change things around. We had Meslier to thank when he was forced to make a save to keep Swansea out. Bamford had a great chance to score after some great build up play between Hernandez and Harrison, but his header was saved by their keeper. The game then ended in spectacular fashion when Ayling went on a long run down the wing and passed the ball across the box. Hernandez struck a peach of a shot into the goal and took off his shirt as he ran to celebrate. When the ball hit the back of the net, Meslier ran the length of the pitch to celebrate with the others, along with all our subs. That was a vital three points and an away win as we get closer to reaching our goal.

LEEDS UNITED V BARNSLEY 16 JULY 2020 AT ELLAND ROAD

With the first of the last three games upon us, I've been trying hard to ignore everything about the forthcoming game, taking each one as it comes. I've still been sharing all my photos from my early days of supporting Leeds to keep my focus elsewhere. No game will be easy for us but as long as we keep fighting until the end, we will have a chance.

Team: Meslier, Ayling, Cooper, White, Costa, Harrison, Klich, Dallas, Berardi, Bamford and Roberts. Subs: Hernandez for Roberts (45), Alioski for Costa (49), Struijk for Harrison (61) and Shackleton for Hernandez (90+3). Leeds won the game 1-0 with an own goal scored by Sollbauer (28). Attendance was 15,000 crowdies and played behind closed doors.

There was a further minute's silence before the game today for Jack Charlton. A big well done to the lads and lasses on the WACCOE forum for their new flag in honour of Big Jack that was on show today. They did one recently for Norman Hunter and Trevor Cherry too and they are both fantastic.

Barnsley, who had ex-Leeds players Mowatt and Halme in the side, had the first opportunity of the game with Meslier called into action. They looked the stronger of the sides, despite them holding the division up in bottom place and looking likely to be relegated. At one time I felt they had double the number of players on the pitch, as there were always loads of red shirts around our players. Klich put a great ball across the box but no one was able to get to it. I said why can't we have them score an own goal as that doesn't seem to happen to us (it shows my memory is rubbish as o.g. was one of our top scorers at one point). I got my wish a few minutes later after some great battling play from Bamford, winning the ball and crossing it into the middle from the byline. The Barnsley player stuck his leg out and put the ball into the net to give us a welcome lead. Despite a couple more chances, that was the score at half-time. We had kept changing formations but were letting Barnsley dictate the play and not able to play to our strengths.

Leeds brought Hernandez on at the break at the same time as Barnsley made a sub, with the latter making an immediate impact, which brought a great save out of Meslier. Within a few minutes of the restart, Costa went down after a challenge from Mowatt at the side of the pitch, with the trainers having to see to him. When he tried getting up, he was in a lot of pain and ended up being stretchered off. With Phillips now being out for the rest of the season due to a knee injury, it didn't look good for Costa, but hopefully it won't be too bad an injury. Berardi brought a save out of their keeper before Barnsley raised their game again. We were struggling to contain Barnsley and the last 30 minutes of the game were torturous and every minute dragged. Along with thousands of other Leeds fans supporting the team from afar, I was willing Leeds to keep the lead and not let Barnsley equalise. With the possession they were having, there was always a danger this could happen. I had my fingers crossed for the last 20 minutes as Leeds finally started to get some space after Barnsley made more substitutions. We nearly got a second goal after great play from Struijk, who put a great ball through to Alioski. His pass put Bamford through, only for their keeper to make a great save to deny him a goal. That would have taken the pressure off us. Instead it was Barnsley who kept attacking and keeping the pressure on us. Meslier was looking very composed and made a great stop from Barnsley to put the ball over for a corner. What a relief it was when the final whistle went as the tension had built up so much that I burst into tears. We are now so close to promotion with only two games left. Please, let it go right for us Leeds as we only need one point to be guaranteed that!

17 JULY 2020 – LEEDS ARE GOING TO THE PREMIER LEAGUE!

Promotion is guaranteed today after Huddersfield Town beat West Bromwich Albion 2-1 and we have now been promoted to the Premier League in our centenary year. As Town scored their second goal at 19.19 it was a sign as Leeds United were formed in 1919. I only watched the last couple of minutes of their game and burst into tears as soon as the final whistle went. The dream we were all waiting for has now become a reality. With videos emerging of fans celebrating at

Elland Road, it made me sad not to be there, but the celebrations are going to be fantastic when we do all get back together at Elland Road. This is for you Norman Hunter, Trevor Cherry and Big Jack Charlton! Marcelo Bielsa and all the players, staff and our wonderful loyal fans, I salute you. 16 years we have waited for this and, despite all the ups and downs, we can finally say United are back!

I had a zoom interview tonight for ITV and will be on BBC Radio Leeds at 7.40am tomorrow as well as Radio 5 Live at 7.15am with this one about crowds coming back to football in October. The latter changed with news of our promotion and that became the focus of the interview. They also had me singing live:

Bielsa, he comes from Argentina, he's come to manage Super Leeds,

They call him El Loco cos he's crazy, he knows exactly what we need,

Ben White at the back, Bamford in attack,

Leeds are going to the Premier League!

I kept singing this over and over again since we were guaranteed promotion, and the last line became the title for this new book. Getting some sleep at the moment though is impossible as I'm wide awake. Just celebrating with our fans on social media has been a special moment. We can go into our last two games needing one point to be champions so let's do it Leeds. I feel there will be a few sore heads amongst our players and staff tomorrow. The pressure is off now though so go and enjoy the last two games and go up in style. LUFC – Marching on Together!

18 JULY 2020 – LEEDS UNITED CROWNED CHAMPIONS OF THE CHAMPIONSHIP!

Wow, what a fantastic two days for Leeds United without even playing, due to results of the two rivals for promotion. Today saw Stoke City beat Brentford, which means neither they nor West Bromwich Albion can catch Leeds, so they are crowned Champions! What a season, now we can relax when we play Derby tomorrow and leave the pressure for automatic promotion to the other two teams.

19 JULY 2020 DERBY COUNTY V LEEDS UNITED AT PRIDE PARK STADIUM

Going into the last two games of the season already promoted as champions was a wonderful feeling. Derby County gave us a guard of honour (it couldn't have happened to a 'nicer' club), as we came out onto the pitch and the team had seven changes to it. With all the celebrations the team and staff have had since knowing we were promoted on Friday night, it wasn't a surprise to see fringe players getting their chance to shine. It was also good to see that the team were allowed to celebrate.

237

Team: Casilla, Douglas, White, Berardi, Struijk. Alioski, Hernandez, Poveda, Dallas, Roberts and Shackleton. Subs: Ayling for Berardi – went off injured with an ACL tear in his knee (33), Harrison for Poveda (77) and Bamford for Roberts (82). Subs not used: Miazek, Cooper, Casey, Davis, Klich and Bogusz. Leeds won 3-1 with goals from Hernandez (56), Shackleton with his first league goal (75) and a Clarke own goal (84). Attendance was zero – behind closed doors.

With no pressure riding on this game, I was looking forward to Leeds playing good football. Roberts had a couple of chances with one over the bar and the other saved by their keeper. Douglas was another to bring a save out of the keeper. Hernandez nearly caught him out when he took a shot from the half-way line, but the keeper got back to save the ball. The game had been a one-way street for most of the game, with Derby limited to sporadic attacks. I thought Poveda had got onto the scoresheet with a well-taken goal only for it to be ruled out for offside. Berardi went down injured and had to be stretchered off, which was a blow. With nine minutes injury time, Leeds continued to put Derby under pressure and Struijk's shot was saved by their keeper.

When the teams came out for the second half it wasn't long before Derby took the lead against the run of play. Luck was on their side when their player found the ball rebound to him in a great position and hit a deflected shot into the net. Luckily for us, Leeds stepped up a gear and hit back straight away after a great run by Poveda. Hernandez received the ball in the penalty area, only for the first shot to be blocked. As the ball rebounded to Hernandez, he made no mistake and stuck the ball in the net to equalise. Roberts nearly got a second shortly afterwards, but with 15 minutes left it was Shackleton who scored with his first goal for the club. I was chuffed to bits for him. Derby tried for an equaliser, but Casilla made the save to keep them out. Leeds then made it three when Alioski sent a great pass into the penalty area, only to see a Derby player stick the ball into the net. That was it, game over, playing our reserves! Dallas brought a save out of their keeper as Leeds ended the game with a win. Leeds have won 27 games this season and set a record number of points with 90.

There were great celebrations on the pitch by the Leeds team as well as Klich leading the singing in the stands. Hopefully, his head isn't too sore from all the celebratory drinks. Seeing a photo of him at Thorpe Arch with his head laid on the bonnet of a car meant it wasn't a surprise to see he was on the subs bench today. Leeds fans were all celebrating in Millennium Square in Leeds too. Our last game of the season that was suspended due to Covid takes place on Wednesday, 22 July against Charlton. Leeds will be presented with the Championship trophy after the game.

LEEDS UNITED V CHARLTON 22 JULY 2020 AT ELLAND ROAD

It was nice going into the last game of the season in the Championship with no pressure and the team able to go out and enjoy playing football. They certainly put on a great display to crown our promotion to the Premier League with Bielsa ball on show and once again Hernandez nutmegging opposition players and showing his class. It was good to see Marcelo Bielsa support the integrity of the competition by putting out a strong team today. Charlton were fighting relegation with ex-Leeds United player Lee Bowyer in charge. As a first for me, I was being mic'd up watching the game at my daughter's house for RMC Sport, French TV. Adam Pope put them in touch with me as they are doing a documentary on Marcelo Bielsa. What I can say is that the infectiousness of supporting Leeds United had rubbed off on Antoine by the time he left us, and he will be supporting them going into the Premier League. Hopefully, we will catch up with him again during the season.

Team: Meslier, Cooper, Dallas, Struijk, Harrison, Alioski, White, Ayling, Hernandez, Bamford and Klich. Subs: Roberts for Bamford (45), Poveda for Alioski (62) and a double substitution of Bogusz for Klich and Stevens for Harrison (73). Leeds won the game 4-0, with goals from White (13), Dallas (28), Roberts (51) and Shackleton (66). Attendance was 15,000 crowdies and played behind closed doors.

Leeds got off to a fantastic start after 13 minutes, when White got the ball on the edge of the box from a corner and struck a fantastic shot straight into the net to put Leeds a goal up. How we cheered, wow, his first goal for the club, and what a goal it was. Leeds were playing some fantastic football as we continued to put pressure on Charlton, with Hernandez having his shot saved by their keeper. Shortly afterwards, Hernandez put a great pass through for Dallas to convert to give us a second goal. Leeds continued to dominate and Ayling and Dallas both had shots saved by their keeper. Charlton looked destined to pull a goal back when they counter-attacked after a Leeds corner, getting past our defence. Meslier came out and put their player off enough for him to send the shot wide. That was one of only a few chances Charlton had on the night. Just before the break, Alioski came close to a further goal but his shot went narrowly wide. That was a good entertaining first half from Leeds as we went into the break two goals up.

In the second half Charlton started off brightly, bringing a save out of Meslier, before Leeds got a third goal. Roberts headed the ball into the net from a corner for another good goal. After a deflected shot from Charlton was saved by Meslier, Leeds got a fourth goal. Struijk sent a great pass out to Poveda to run down the wing, who then passed the ball into the middle for Shackleton to get his second goal in two games. Ayling brought another save out of their keeper then Meslier was called into action again but we were able to keep another clean sheet. Leeds ended the game on the attack with an emphatic victory over Charlton.

Leeds had asked fans to stay away from the ground but there were thousands already there with fireworks going off at half-time. We had originally planned to go over after the game but had changed our minds when we heard news that Leeds would ban fans if they went there. With social media posts saying there was an open-top bus there, I knew they were going to end the filming for the documentary. When Antoine asked at 10pm if we were going to the ground as he wanted to film there, we made the on-the-spot decision to go as soon as Leeds were presented with the trophy. It was fantastic seeing Leeds get the Championship trophy before heading off for Elland Road with Antoine following us. We'd just got parked up and were walking to the ground as we heard cheers and knew we had missed the team on the bus. Fans were already streaming away from the ground as we headed to the start of Lowfields Road near Billy's statue, being careful not to go into the middle of the crowd. The smell from the flares was awful and I was glad I had my Leeds United mask on. I did an interview outside the ground for Antoine and he was happy to get footage of Bielsa flags and fans celebrating for his documentary. I was glad we'd made the effort to go, despite not seeing the team, because it was important to be a part of it. We'd waited 16 years for this moment and I know many fans who did adhere to the stay at home message were very upset not to be at the ground and see it for themselves rather than from videos. That is understandable, especially as many of those I know go home and away to follow Leeds. News had been filtering through social media channels all day that the team would be going onto the bus, so it was always going to happen. In their defence, I do feel that Leeds had to adhere to the stay at home message and follow protocol, which was the only reason they said it.

After all the worries about being in a three-horse race, Leeds ended up ten points clear of West Bromwich Albion (WBA) in second place, who also gained automatic promotion. Brentford succumbed to the pressure, made do with the play-offs and got to the final with Fulham to decide the third place for promotion. Fulham won the final to gain the final promotion slot. Interestingly, WBA have got promoted with the same number of points Leeds had last year, which put us in the play-offs. Once the pressure was off, Leeds showed how good they could play, which culminated in a club record of 93 points and a goal difference of 42.

CHAPTER 12

FIXTURES AND RESULTS
SEASON 2019-20 – 54 GAMES AND FINAL COMMENTS

My final comments in my book *Marcelo Bielsa's Leeds United* last year stated the following:

My ambition last year was to aim for automatic promotion, which we came so close to doing. This year I want exactly the same but for us to gain promotion in our centenary year. Have high aspirations and you have a better chance of achieving your aim.

Leeds United achieved those aspirations, have done it and got promoted to the Premier League as champions! Well done Leeds on making the dream of promotion a reality, and thank you Marcelo Bielsa for the best football we have seen for years. I am positive he will sign a new contract to take us forward and show the Premier League what they have been missing. I love his integrity, honesty and dedication to play the game the way I want to see it. Having players who never give up, wear the Leeds shirt with pride and want to play for us has been a revelation and something that has been missing for many years.

Meslier and Costa have now signed new deals to stay permanently with the club after their loan periods were up. Ben White, you know you love it at Leeds and there is no better club for you to be at! I expect the nucleus of the side to be staying, with maybe a few additions as well as some of our youngsters coming through. By making sure everyone plays the same way, they can be introduced into the first team and adapt easily.

For our fans who show their love and loyalty by following Leeds United all over the world, I look forward to catching up with you at Premier League games next season. For those of you who have been following my old photos, my blogs and love having your photos taken, I thank you for your unconditional support. My blog and photos give a pictorial version of following our team to the Premier League so enjoy the journey. Our support is phenomenal, which I love being part of, and I cannot wait for the start of the season and being able to go back to Elland Road.

See you soon, LUFC – Marching on Together!

DATE	OPPOSITION	VENUE	COMPETITION	SCORE	ATT	SCORERS
10.7.19	York City	Bootham Crescent	Pre-season friendly	0-5	5,108 with 2,162 Leeds fans	Harrison 3, 44 Roofe 22 Hernandez 34 Forshaw 53
11.7.19	Guiseley	Nethermoor Park	Pre-season friendly	1-2	5,000 approx.	Costa 69 Bogusz 80
17.7.19	man utd	Optus stadium in Perth, Australia	Australia Pre-season tour Did not attend	0-4	55,274	
20.7.19	Western Sydney Wanderers	Official opening of the new Bankwest stadium In Sydney, Australia	Australia Pre-season tour Did not attend	1-2	24,419	Bogusz 9 Hernandez 90+5
27.7.19	Cagliari	Sardegna arena Sardinia, Italy	Italy Pre-season friendly Did not attend	1-1		Hernandez (pen) 49
4.8.19	Bristol City	Ashton Gate	Championship	1-3	23,553 with Approx. 2,300 Leeds fans	Hernandez 26 Bamford 57 Harrison 72
10.8.19	Nottingham Forest	Elland Road	Championship	1-1	35,453 2,001 Forest fans	Hernandez 59
13.8.19	Salford City	Peninsula Stadium	Carabao Cup 1st round	0-3	5,108 1,400 Leeds fans	Nketiah 43 Berardi 50 Klich 58
17.8.19	Wigan	DW Stadium	Championship	0-2	14,819 5,200 Leeds fans	Bamford 34, 65
21.8.19	Brentford	Elland Road	Championship	1-0	35,004 Approx. 300 Brentford fans	Nketiah 81
24.8.19	Stoke	Bet365 Stadium	Championship	0-3	24,090 2,913 Leeds fans	Dallas 42 Alioski 50 Bamford 66
27.8.19	Stoke	Elland Road	Carabao Cup 2nd round	2-2 full time Leeds lost 5-4 on penalties	30,002 811 Stoke fans	Nketiah 67 Costa 81 Penalties: Douglas, Costa, Phillips, Nketiah Harrison's penalty hit the post so Stoke went through
31.8.19	Swansea City	Elland Road	Championship	0-1	Attendance 34,935 1,418 Swansea fans	
15.9.19	Barnsley	Oakwell	Championship	0-2	Attendance 17,598 4,400 Leeds fans	Nketiah 84 Klich (pen) 89
21.9.19	Derby	Elland Road	Championship	1-1	34,714 1,024 Derby fans	Lowe own goal 29
28.9.19	Charlton	The Valley	Championship	1-0	21,808 3,179 Leeds fans	
1.10.19	West Bromwich Albion	Elland Road	Championship	1-0	34,648 981 WBA fans	Alioski 38
5.10.19	Millwall	The Den	Championship	2-1	16,311 2,221 Leeds fans	Alioski 46

DATE	OPPOSITION	VENUE	COMPETITION	SCORE	ATT	SCORERS
19.10.19	Birmingham	Elland Road	Championship	1-0	35,731 1,996 Birmingham fans	Phillips 65
22.10.19	Preston	Deepdale	Championship	1-1	18,275 5,648 Leeds fans	Nketiah 87
26.10.19	Sheffield Wednesday	Hillsborough	Championship	0-0	27,516 Approx. 4,500 Leeds fans	
2.11.19	QPR	Elland Road	Championship	2-0	35,284 1,093 QPR fans	Roberts 39 Harrison 82
9.11.19	Blackburn Rovers	Elland Road	Championship	2-1	35,567 973 Blackburn fans	Bamford (pen) 30 Harrison 35
23.11.19	Luton	Kenilworth Road	Championship	1-2	10,068 1,035 Leeds fans	Bamford 51, 90
26.11.19	Reading	Madejski Stadium	Championship	0-1	16,918 2,050 Leeds fans	Harrison 87
30.11.19	Middlesbrough	Elland Road	Championship	4-0	35,626 1,806 Boro fans	Bamford 3 Klich 45+3, 73 Costa 67
7.12.19	Huddersfield	John Smith's Stadium	Championship	0-2	23,805 2,314 Leeds fans	Alioski 50 Hernandez 78
10.12.19	Hull City	Elland Road	Championship	2-0	35,200 1,512 Hull fans	De Wijs own goal 73 Alioski 82
14.12.19	Cardiff City	Elland Road	Championship	3-3	34,552 710 Cardiff fans	Costa 6 Bamford 8 & (pen) 52
21.12.19	Fulham	Craven Cottage	Championship	2-1	18,878 Approx. 1,900 Leeds fans	Bamford 54
26.12.19	Preston	Elland Road	Championship	1-1	35,638 805 Preston fans	Dallas 89
29.12.19	Birmingham	St Andrew's Trillion Trophy Stadium	Championship	4-5	22,059 Approx. 2,000 Leeds fans	Costa 15 Harrison 21 Ayling 69 Dallas 84 Harding own goal 90+5
1.1.20	West Bromwich Albion	The Hawthorns	Championship	1-1	25,618 1,989 Leeds fans	Bamford 52
6.1.20	Arsenal	The Emirates	FA Cup 3rd round	1-0	58,403 8,000 Leeds fans	
11.1.20	Sheffield Wednesday	Elland Road	Championship	0-2	36,422 2,644 Sheff Wed fans	
18.1.20	QPR	Kiyan Prince Foundation Stadium	Championship	1-0	16,049 2,973 Leeds fans	
28.1.20	Millwall	Elland Road	Championship	3-2	34,006 471 Millwall fans	Bamford 48,66 Hernandez 62
1.2.20	Wigan	Elland Road	Championship	0-1	35,162 519 Wigan fans	

DATE	OPPOSITION	VENUE	COMPETITION	SCORE	ATT	SCORERS
8.2.20	Nottingham Forest	City Ground	Championship	2-0	29,455 1,993 Leeds fans	
11.2.20	Brentford	Griffin Park (last game there)	Championship	1-1	12,294 1,400 Leeds fans	Cooper 39
15.2.20	Bristol City	Elland Road	Championship	1-0	35,819 1,203 Bristol fans	Ayling 16
22.2.20	Reading	Elland Road	Championship	1-0	35,483 806 Reading fans	Hernandez 57
26.2.20	Middlesbrough	The Riverside	Championship	0-1	24,647 4,400 Leeds fans	Klich 45+1
29.2.20	Hull City	KCOM Stadium	Championship	0-4	16,178 3,519+ Leeds fans	Ayling 5 Hernandez 47 Roberts 81,84
7.3.20	Huddersfield	Elland Road	Championship	2-0	36,514 2,647 Town fans	Ayling 3 Bamford 51
21.6.20	Cardiff City	Cardiff City Stadium	Championship	2-0	No fans behind closed doors	
27.6.20	Fulham	Elland Road	Championship	3-0	No fans behind closed doors 15,000 crowdies	Bamford 10 Alioski 56 Harrison 71
30.6.20	Luton	Elland Road	Championship	1-1	No fans behind closed doors 15,000 crowdies	Dallas 65
4.7.20	Blackburn	Ewood Park	Championship	1-3	No fans behind closed doors	Bamford 7 Phillips 40 Klich 53
9.7.20	Stoke City	Elland Road	Championship	5-0	No fans behind closed doors 15,000 crowdies	Klich (pen) 45 Costa 47 Cooper 57 Hernandez 72 Bamford 90+3
12.7.20	Swansea	Liberty Stadium	Championship	0-1	No fans behind closed doors	Hernandez 89
16.7.20	Barnsley	Elland Road	Championship	1-0	No fans behind closed doors 15,000 crowdies	Sollbauer own goal. 28
19.7.20	Derby County	The Pride Park Stadium	Championship	1-3	No fans behind closed doors	Hernandez 56 Shackleton 75 Clarke own goal 84
22.7.20	Charlton	Elland Road	Championship	4-0	No fans behind closed doors 15,000 crowdies	White 13 Dallas 28 Roberts 51 Shackleton 66

LEEDS UNITED PROMOTED TO THE PREMIER LEAGUE IN THEIR CENTENARY SEASON 2019-2020

The final table on 22 July 2020 after the last game of the season, showing Leeds with pride of place at the top of the league!

CHAMPIONSHIP TABLE 2019-20

POS	TEAM	P	W	D	L	F	A	GD	PTS
1	**LEEDS UNITED**	46	28	9	9	77	35	42	93
2	WEST BROMWICH ALBION	46	22	17	7	77	45	32	83
3	BRENTFORD	46	24	9	13	80	38	42	81
4	FULHAM	46	23	12	11	64	48	16	81
5	CARDIFF CITY	46	19	16	11	68	58	10	73
6	SWANSEA CITY	46	18	16	12	62	53	9	70
7	NOTTINGHAM FOREST	46	18	16	12	58	50	8	70
8	MILLWALL	46	17	17	12	57	51	6	68
9	PRESTON	46	18	12	16	59	54	5	66
10	DERBY COUNTY	46	17	13	16	62	64	-2	64
11	BLACKBURN ROVERS	46	17	12	17	66	63	3	63
12	BRISTOL CITY	46	17	12	17	60	65	-5	63
13	QUEENS PARK RANGERS	46	16	10	20	67	76	-9	58
14	READING FC	46	15	11	20	59	58	1	56
15	STOKE CITY	46	16	8	22	62	68	-6	56
16	SHEFFIELD WEDNESDAY	46	15	11	20	58	66	-8	56
17	MIDDLESBROUGH	46	13	14	19	48	61	-13	53
18	HUDDERSFIELD TOWN	46	13	12	21	52	70	-18	51
19	LUTON TOWN	46	14	9	23	54	82	-28	51
20	BIRMINGHAM CITY	46	12	14	20	54	75	-21	50
21	BARNSLEY	46	12	13	21	49	69	-20	49
22	CHARLTON ATHLETIC	46	12	12	22	50	65	-15	48
23	WIGAN	46	15	14	17	57	56	1	47
24	HULL CITY	46	12	9	25	57	87	-30	45

ND - #0200 - 270225 - C0 - 234/156/11 - PB - 9781780916156 - Gloss Lamination